TAI DAVIS

[Pastry]

[A Visual Anthology of Culinary Works]

Bailey Girls Publishing, LLC

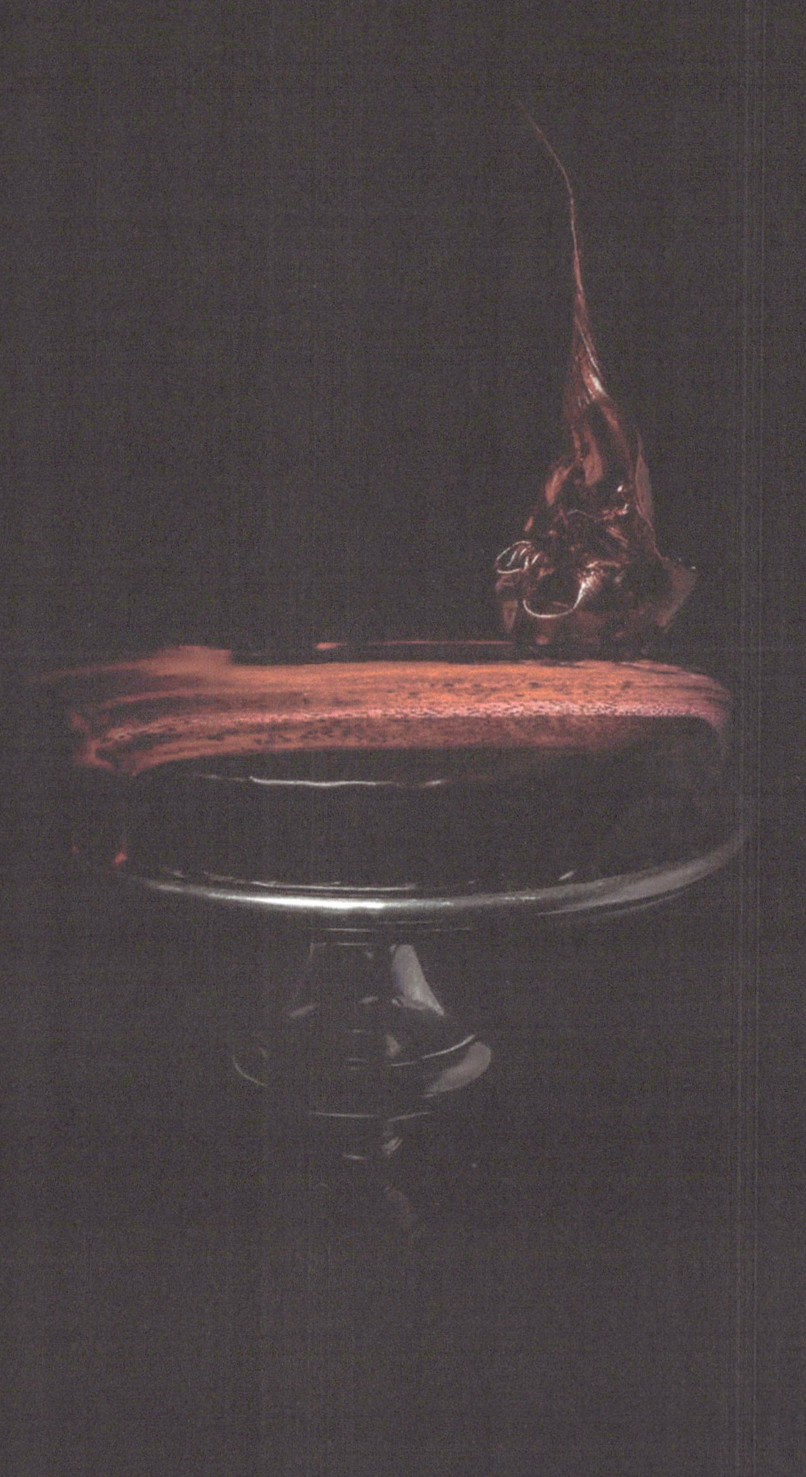

TAI DAVIS

[Pastry]

Visual Anthology of Culinary Works

By Chef Tai Davis

ISBN: 978-1-942037-07-1

First Edition

Library of Congress Control Number: 2019916980

Library of Congress Cataloging-in-Publication

Davis, Tyler

Tai Davis: Pastry, A visual anthology of culinary works/ By Tai Davis

p.cm 8.5 x 8.5

ISBN: 978-1-942037-07-1

1. Pastry 2. Art 3. Desserts

Photography by Tai Davis, Judd Demaline, Izaiah Johnson

Wes Law, Eric Nemens, Jonathan Pollack and Mabel Suen

Printed in the United States

Published in Saint Louis, MO, United States

Bailey Girls Publishing, LLC

www.baileygirls.com

Book design by Tai Davis

This book is dedicated to all the individuals who inspire, support, and nurture my spirit. Thank you for your endless light. wisdom and love.

Namaste

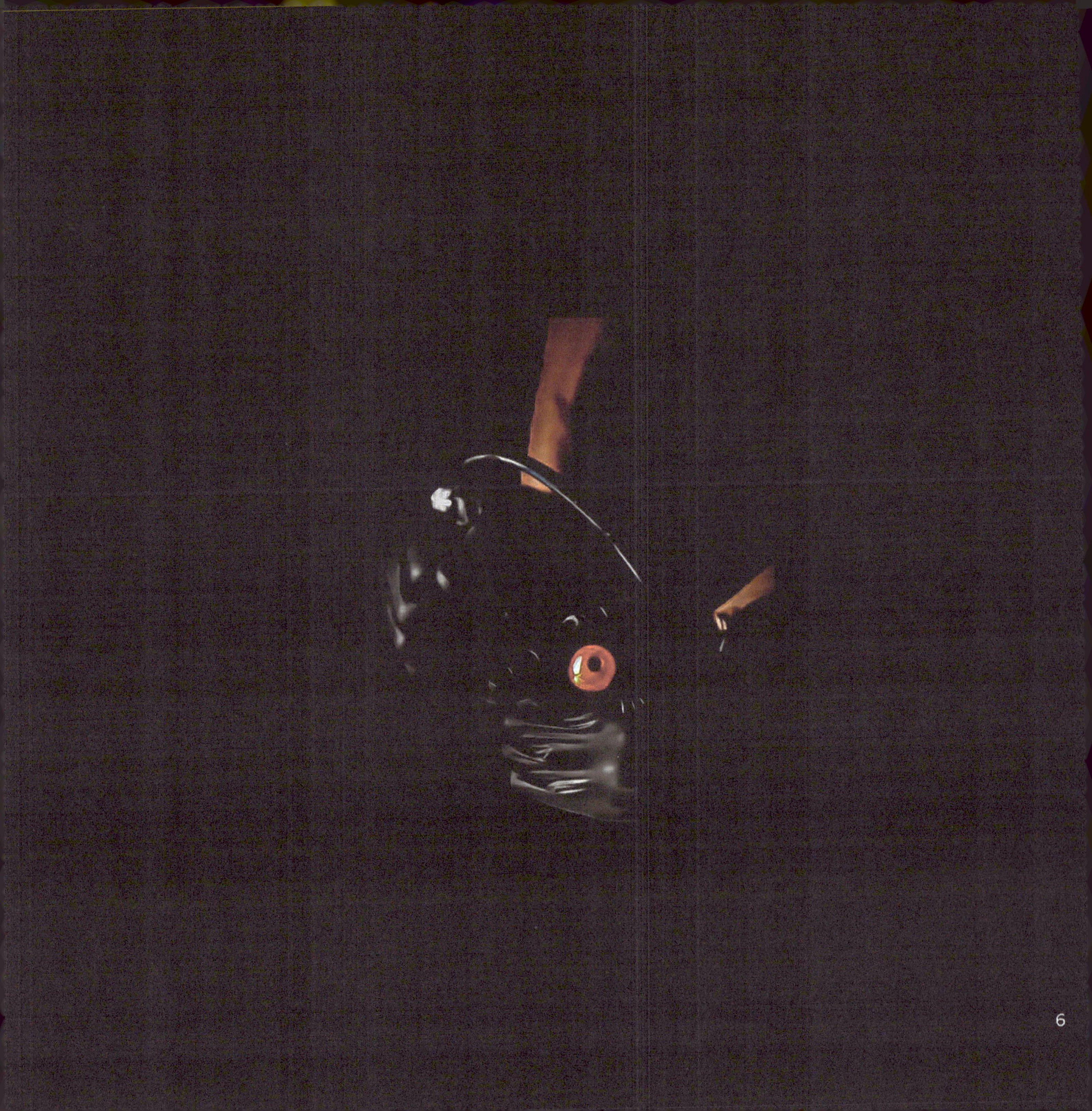

Forward

Have you ever eaten something so magnificent that it evokes an overwhelming emotion? Maybe it triggers a pleasant memory from childhood or reminds you of some special dish a beloved family member used to make. Or perhaps it's completely new to you and as you're enjoying it you're creating an altogether new memory.

I distinctly remember one of the first dessert I had by Tyler. It was in 2015 at a small restaurant/art space in St. Louis, The Tavern of the Fine Arts, which is now closed. Truth be told, I'm not a huge fan of sweets but when I saw a deconstructed s'mores on the menu, I knew I had to try it. You see, growing up my family would often spend weekends at our country house in the middle of the woods in southern Missouri and most nights there we would build a fire and make s'mores. These are now some of my most cherished memories: the smell of the smoke, my grandma's laughter, the stars, the calm of the woods, anticipating the call of the whippoorwill. And with one simple dish, Tyler was able to bring all those memories rushing back. In my opinion, this is what makes Tyler's dishes so special - he creates from the heart.

After The Tavern, we followed him to Brennan's where he would create coursed meals at their Purveyor's Table. It was an intimate setting at a large table where the chef would cook dishes in front of you and tell stories about the food as they were cooking. Tyler always had the best narratives for his diners, and since he was creating based off his beloved memories, guests were never disappointed. I personally was elated when he brought back a version of the deconstructed s'mores at one of the dinners because I could once again relive my days at the country house.

His next big adventure was with the Chocolate Pig where he had free reign to create whatever desserts he wanted. Guests could even sit at the dessert station to watch and interact with the pastry chef as he confidently prepared dishes. I was fortunate to have sat there a few times and watch Tyler work his magic. There were many times when I had no idea what he was putting on the plate but I didn't care because whatever he constructed was always sensational. Whether it was a combo of sweet and salty, tart and fruity, or the signature peanut butter bomb (which was itself a production of melting chocolate) - you knew you were in expert culinary hands with Tyler.

-Becca Francis

Contents

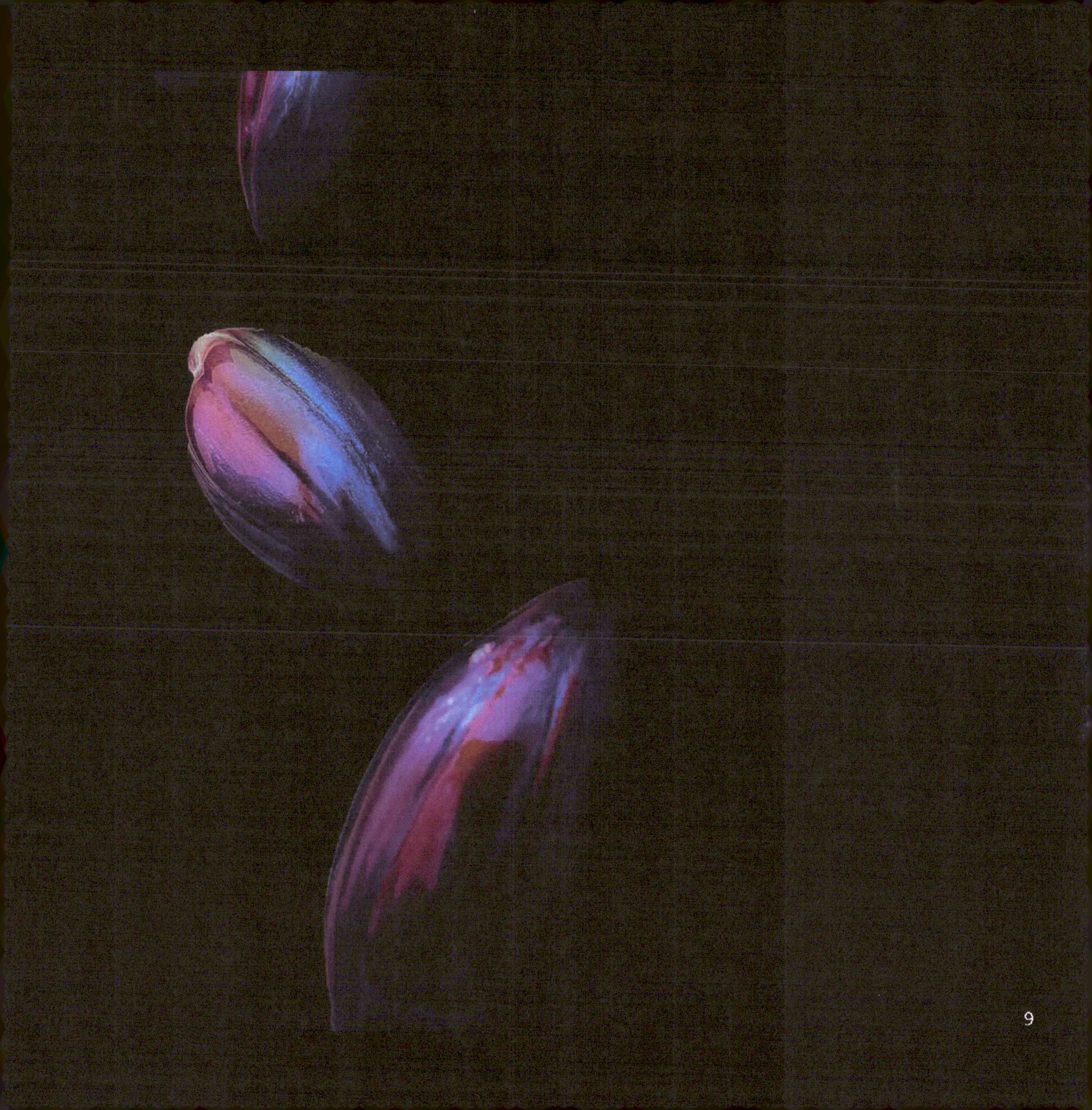

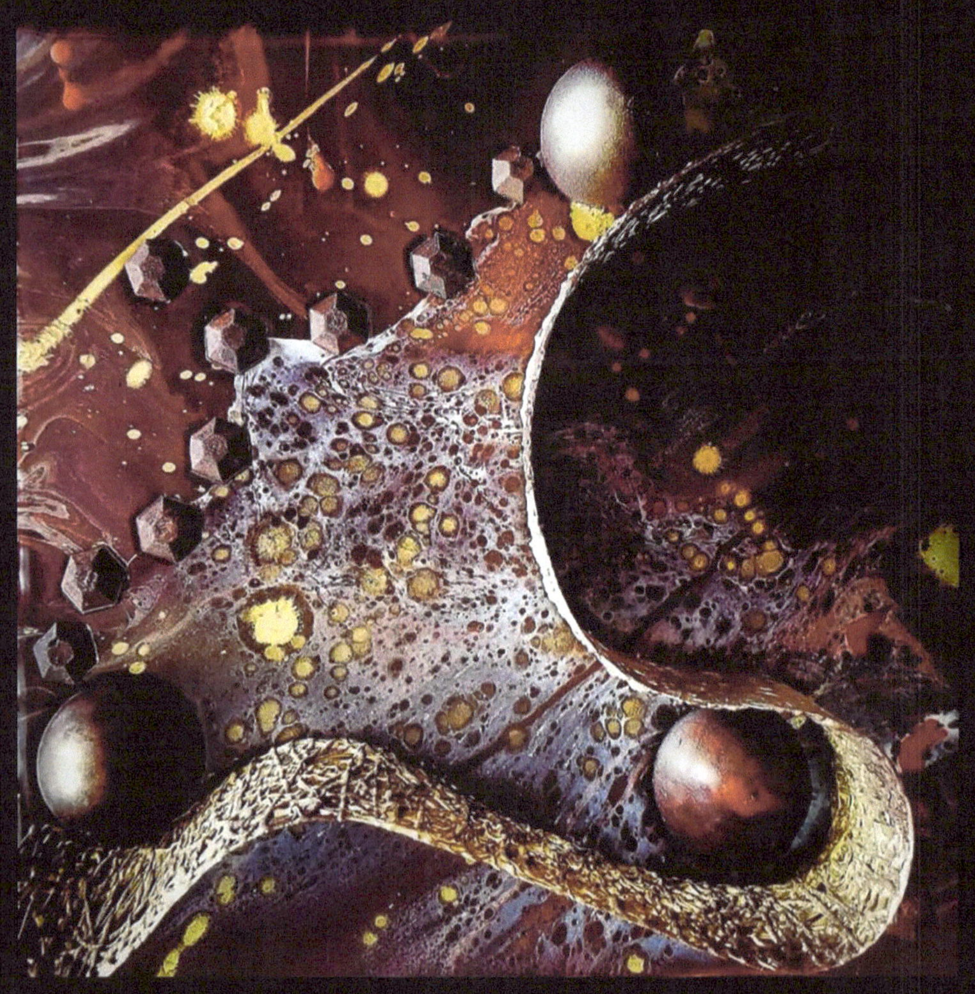

Chocolate, Bourbon-Salted Caramel

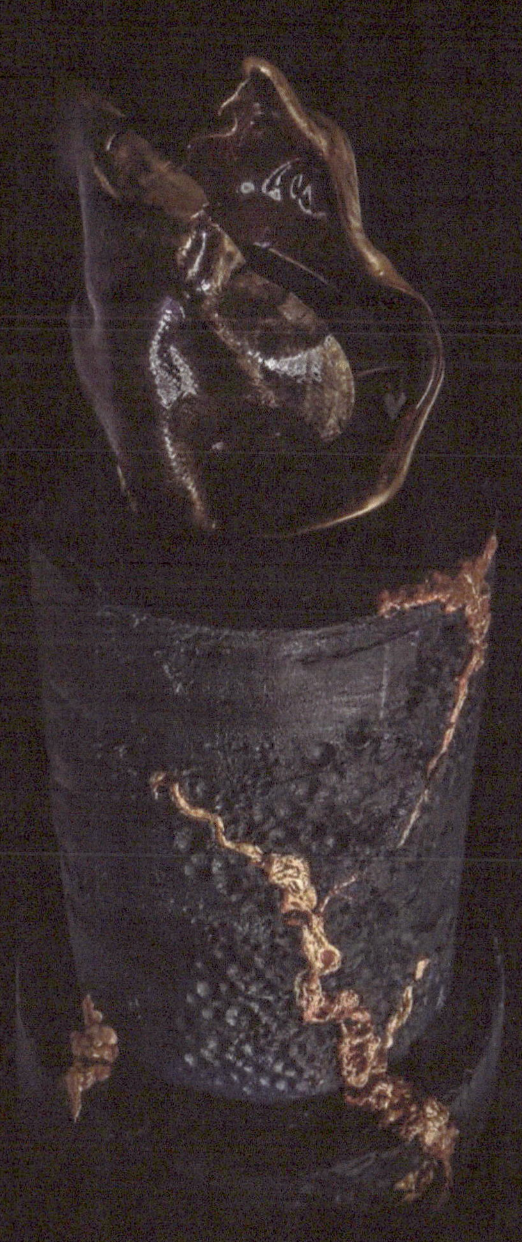

Earth Cake Fig.1

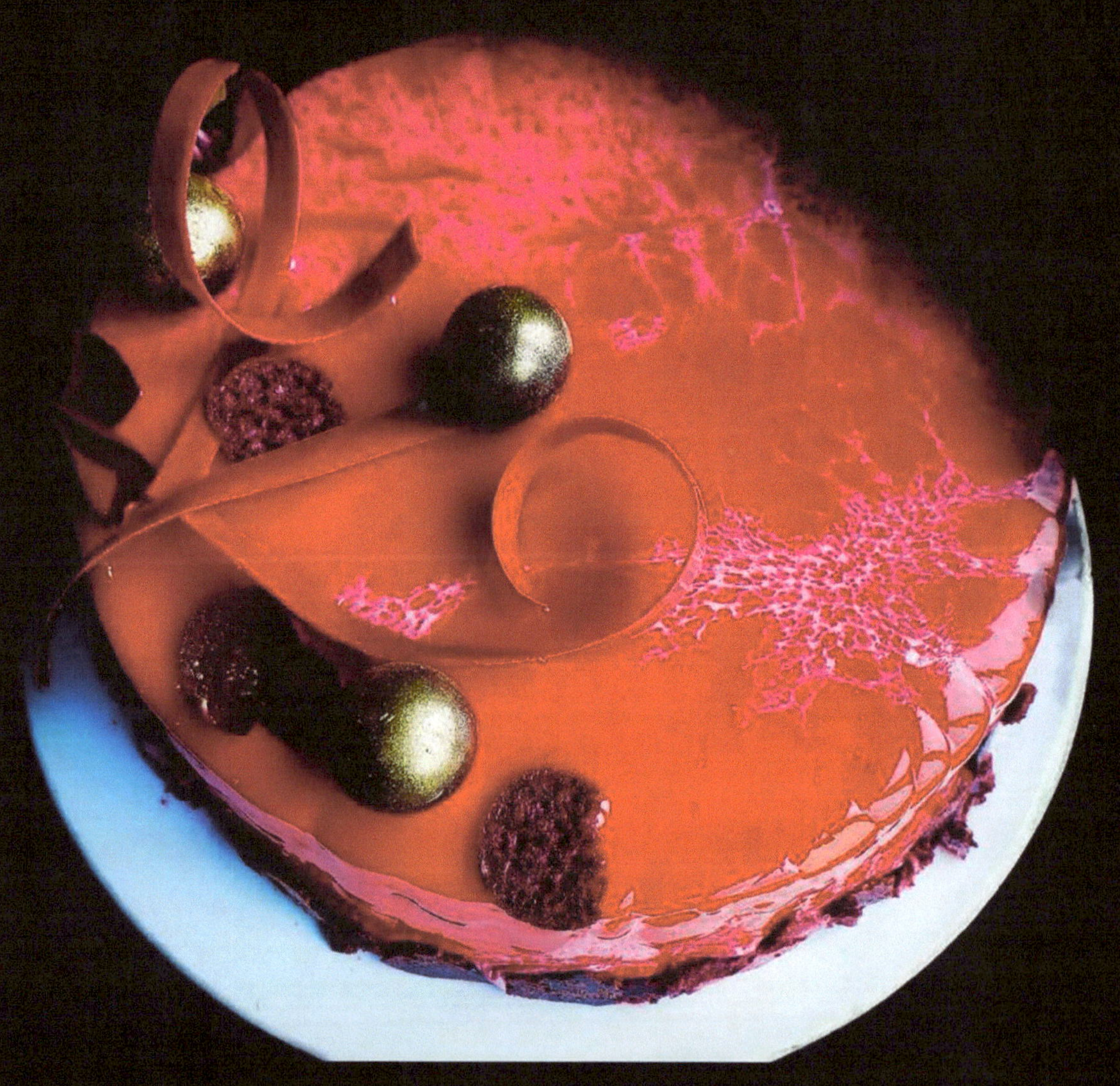

Strawberry, Passionfruit, and "Fraise" Chocolate *'Amore'*

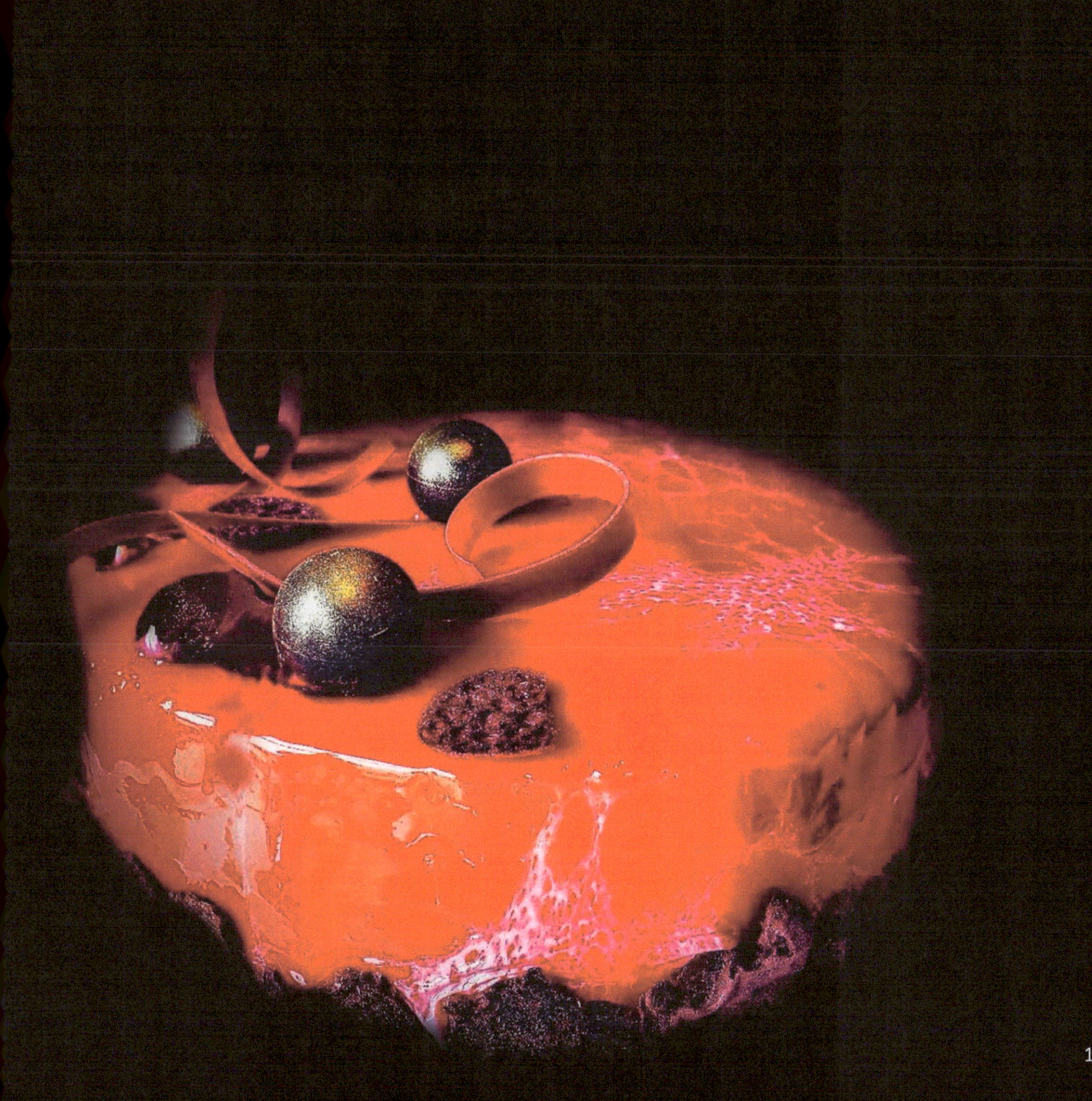

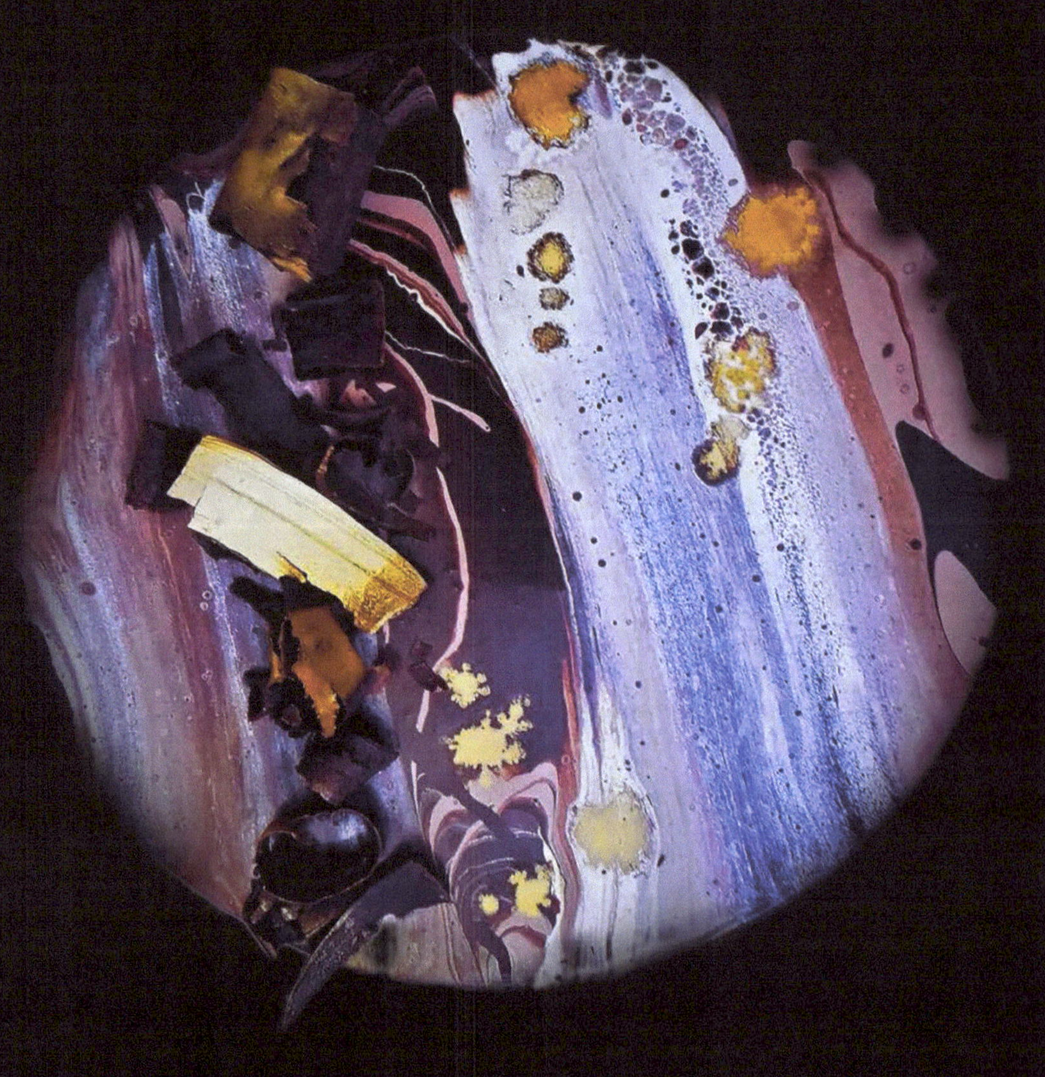

Tiramisu Cheesecake

'Your work is to discover your work – and then with all your heart to give yourself to it.'

[Buddha]

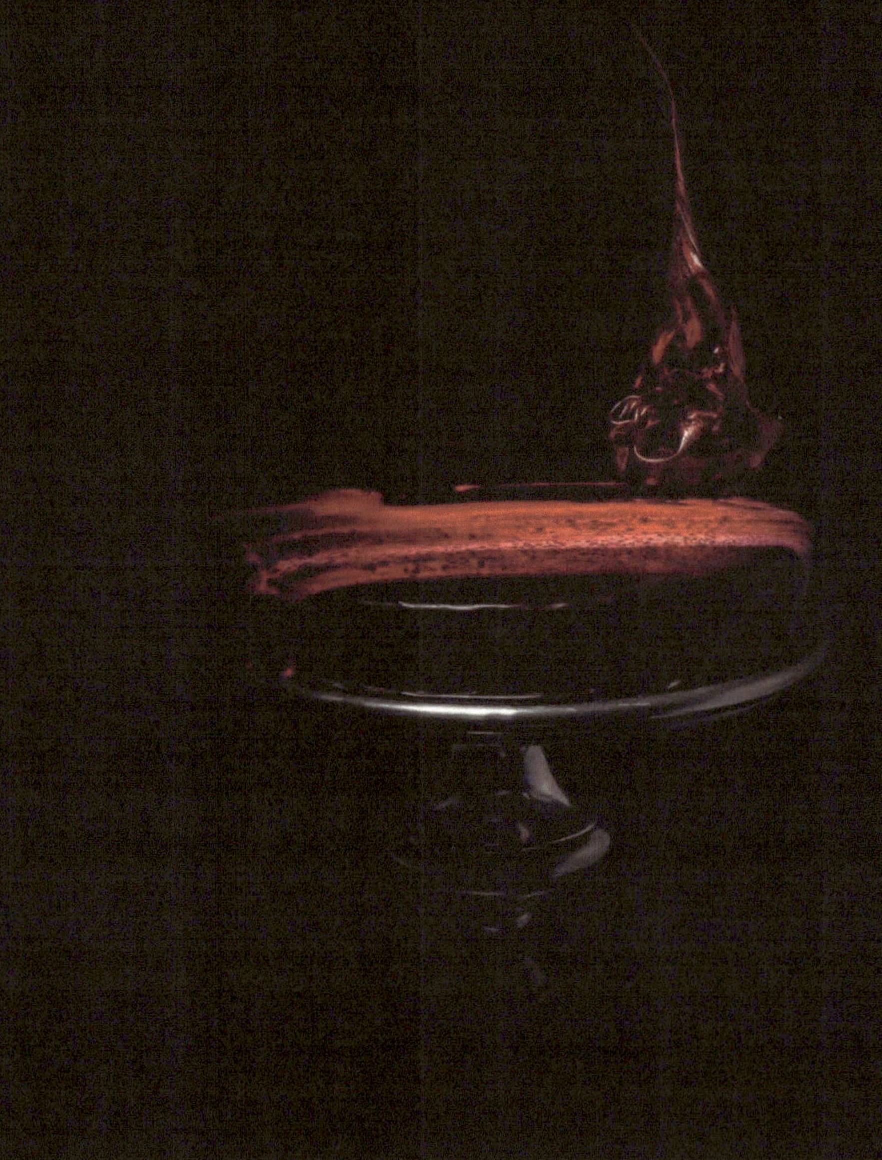

Chocolate Habanero

Fire Cake Fig. 1

'Lust'

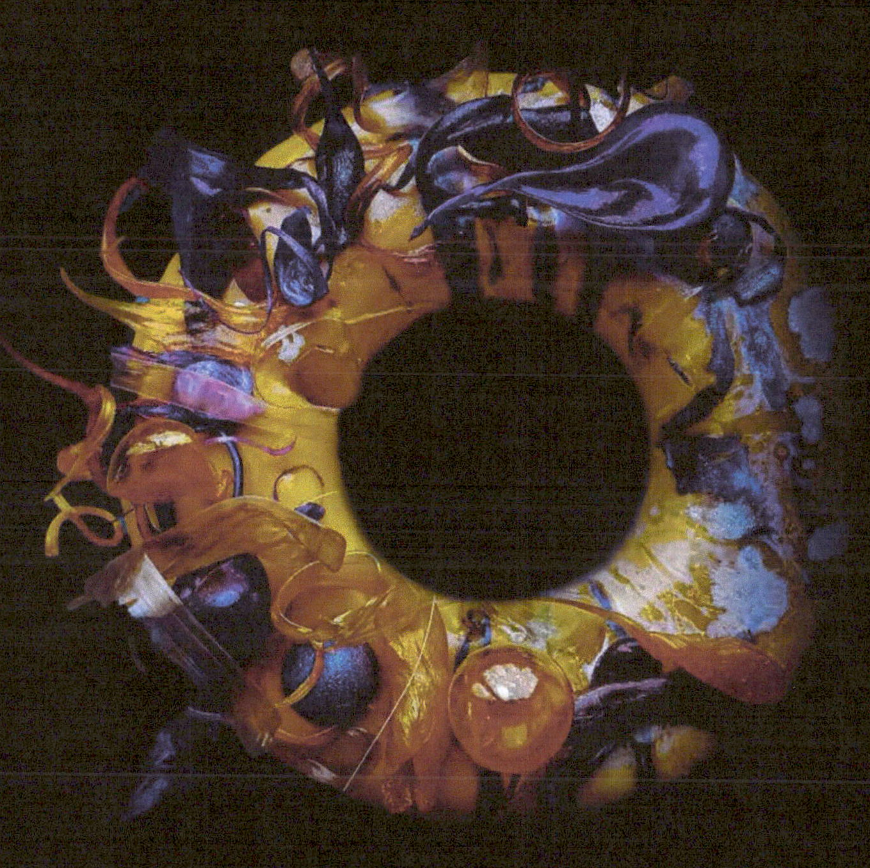

Mango, Almond, Blackberry

'Chihuly

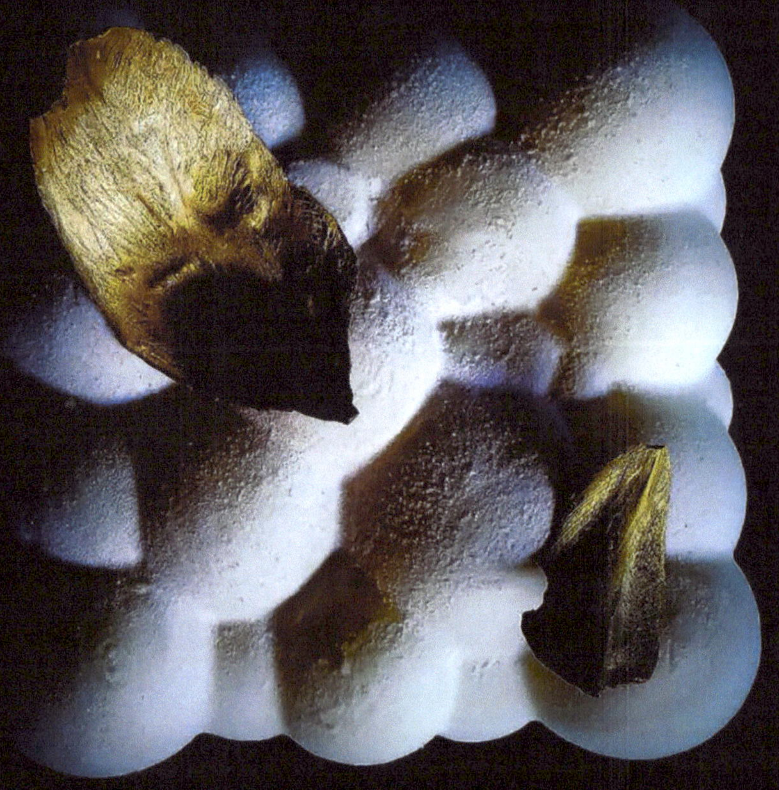

White Chocolate, Lychee, Vanilla Entremet

Air Fig. 1

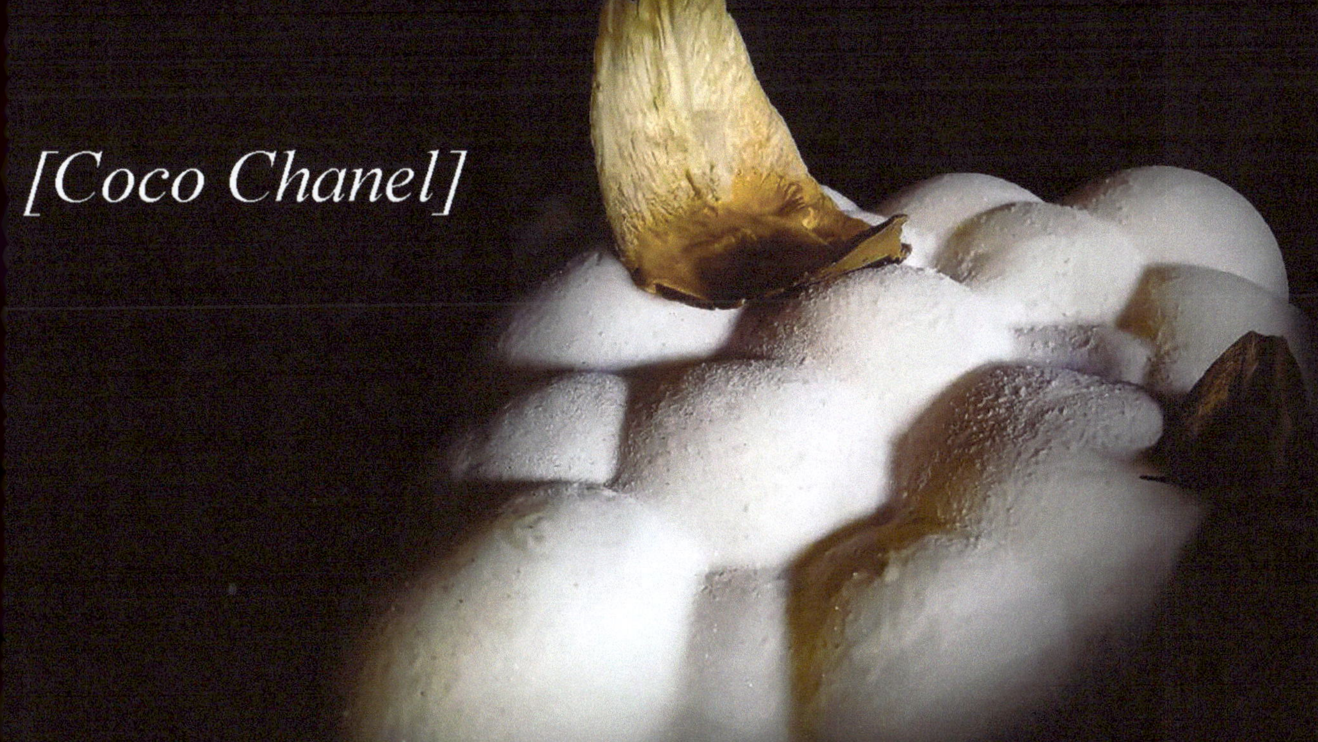

"If you were born without wings, do nothing to prevent them from growing."

[Coco Chanel]

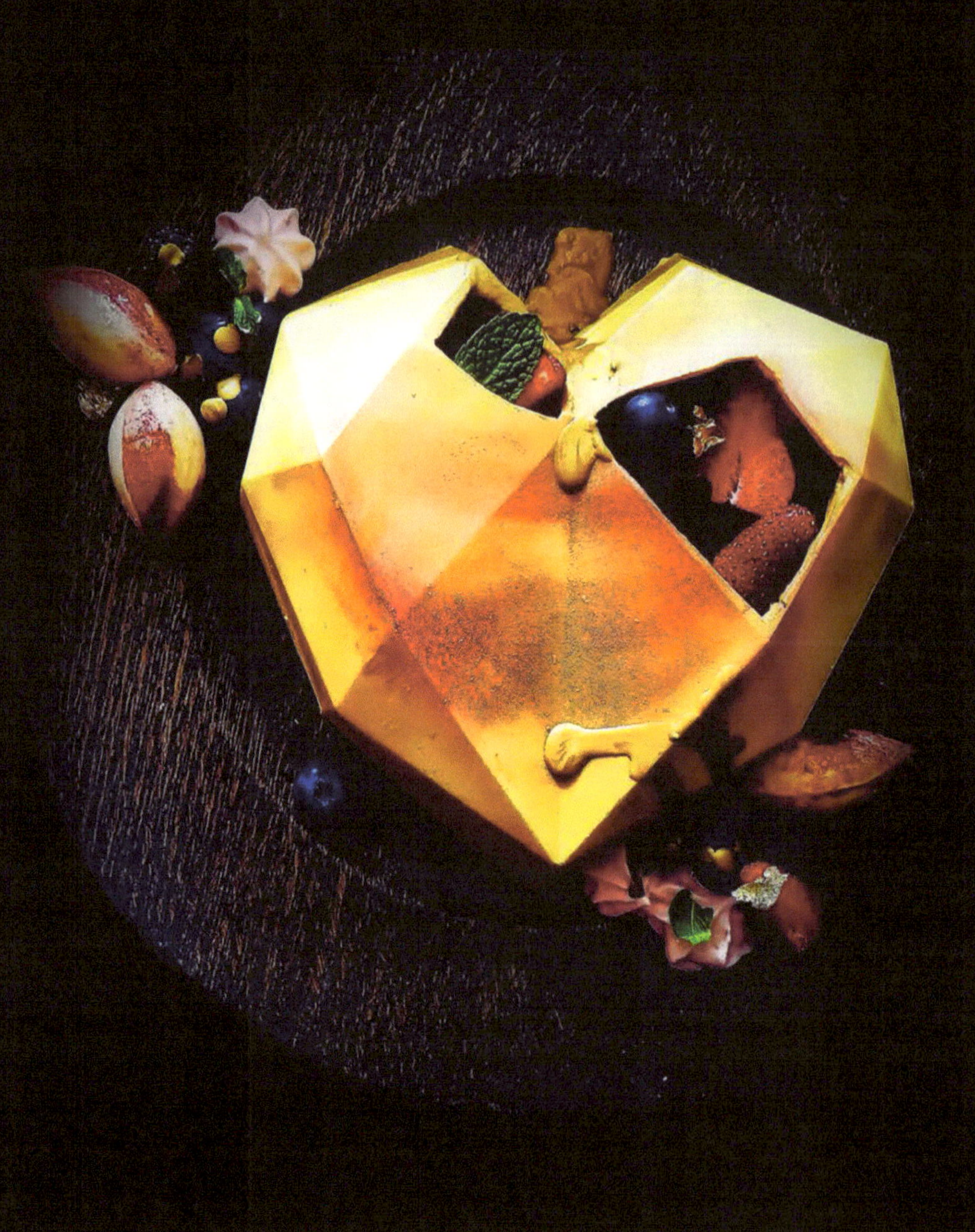

Passion fruit, Raspberry, Green Strawberry, Oats

'Passionate Heart'

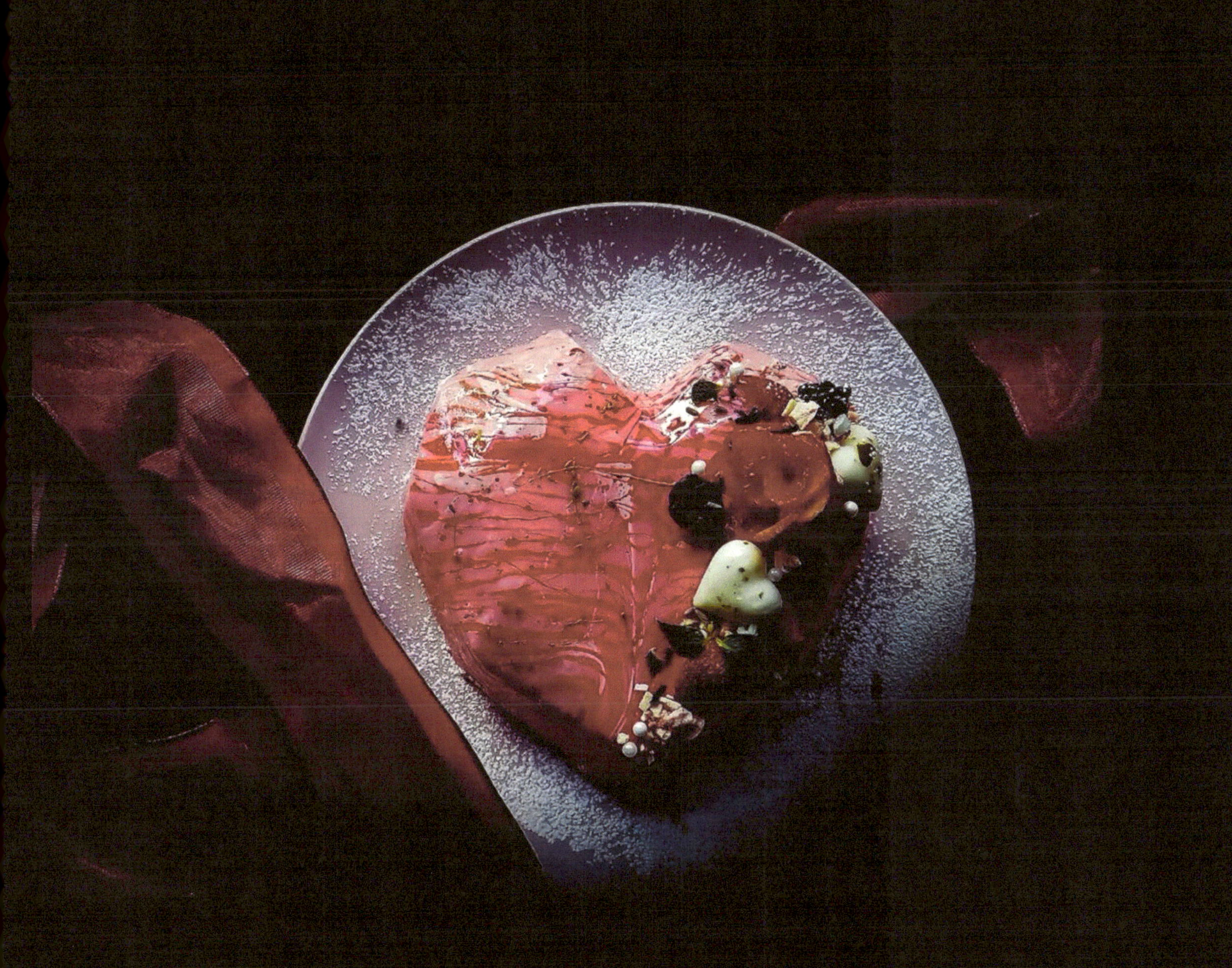

Strawberry Cheesecake, White Chocolate, Rose

'Sacred Heart'

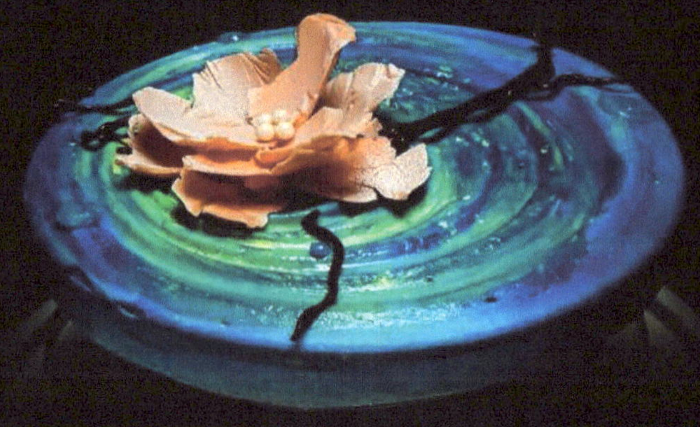

Elderflower, Blueberry, White Chocolate

Water Fig. 1

'Buddha'

22

'Love of beauty is Taste. The creation of beauty is Art'

[R.W.Emerson]

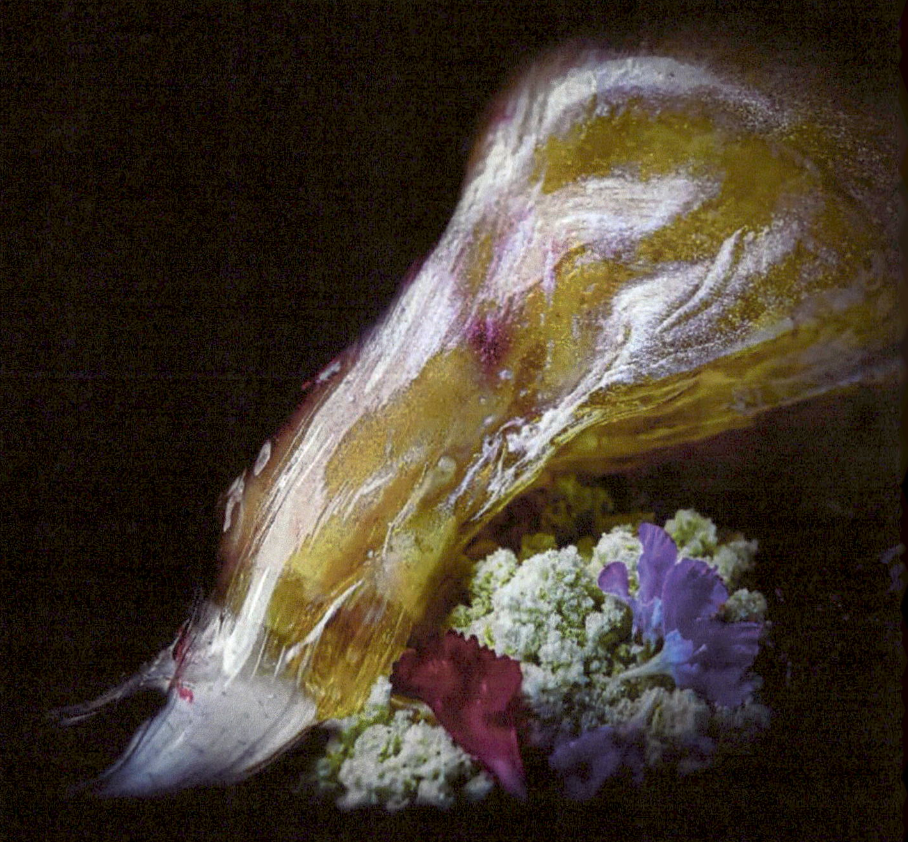

Beet, Tarragon, Goat Cheese, Hibiscus

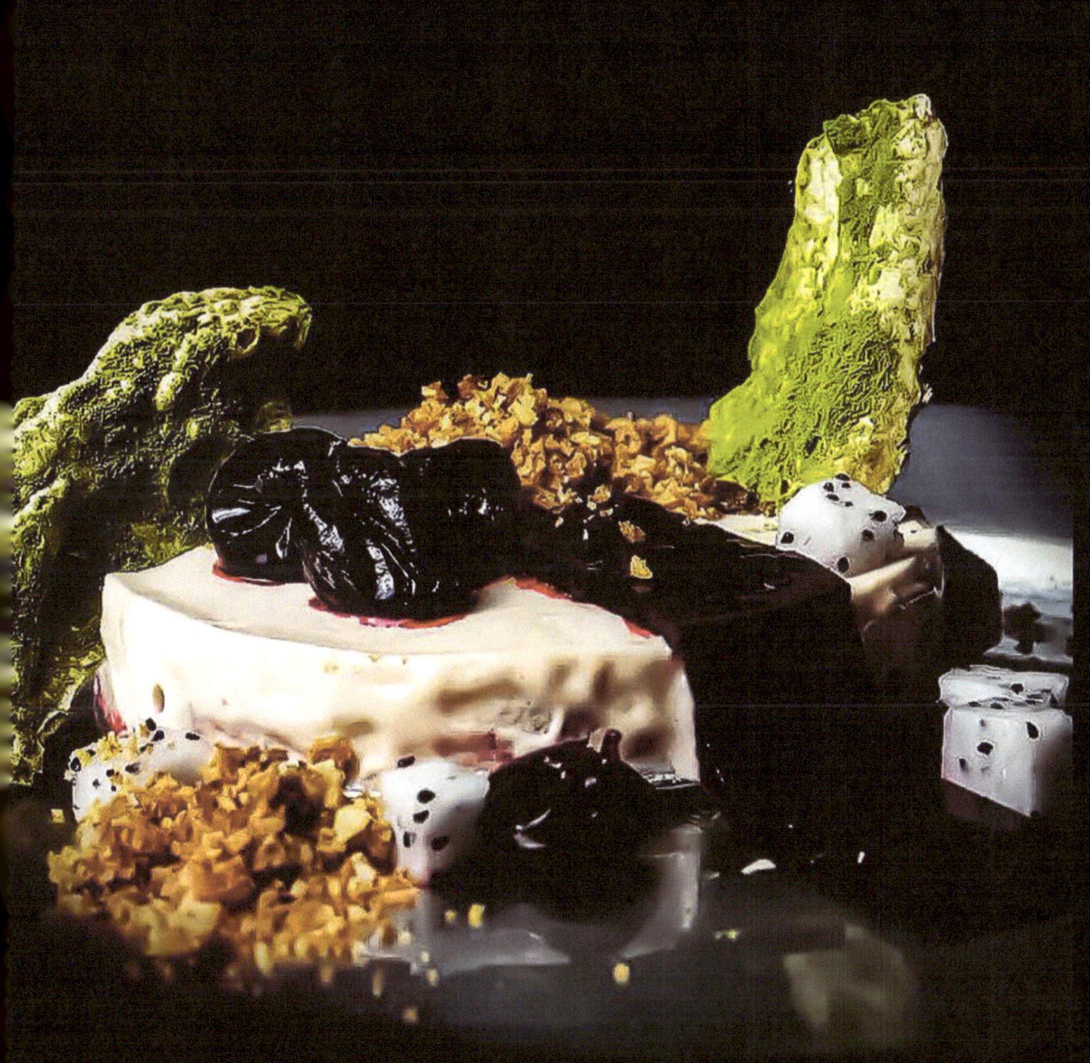

Dragon fruit, Matcha, Black Cherry, Miso

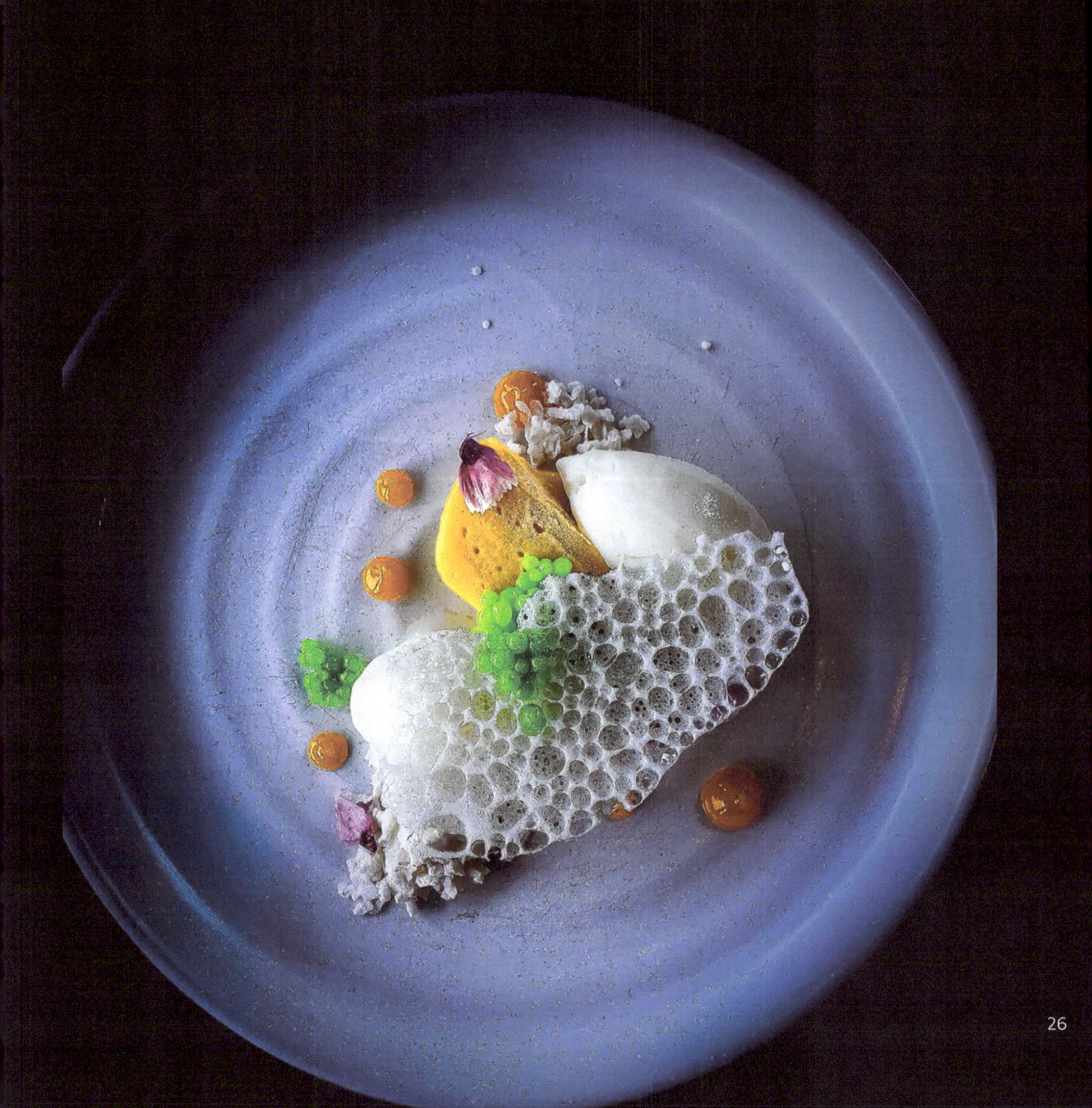

'La bonne cuisine est la base du véritable bonheur.'

[Escoffier]

Mango, Yoghurt, Finger Lime, Coconut

'Mango Lassi'

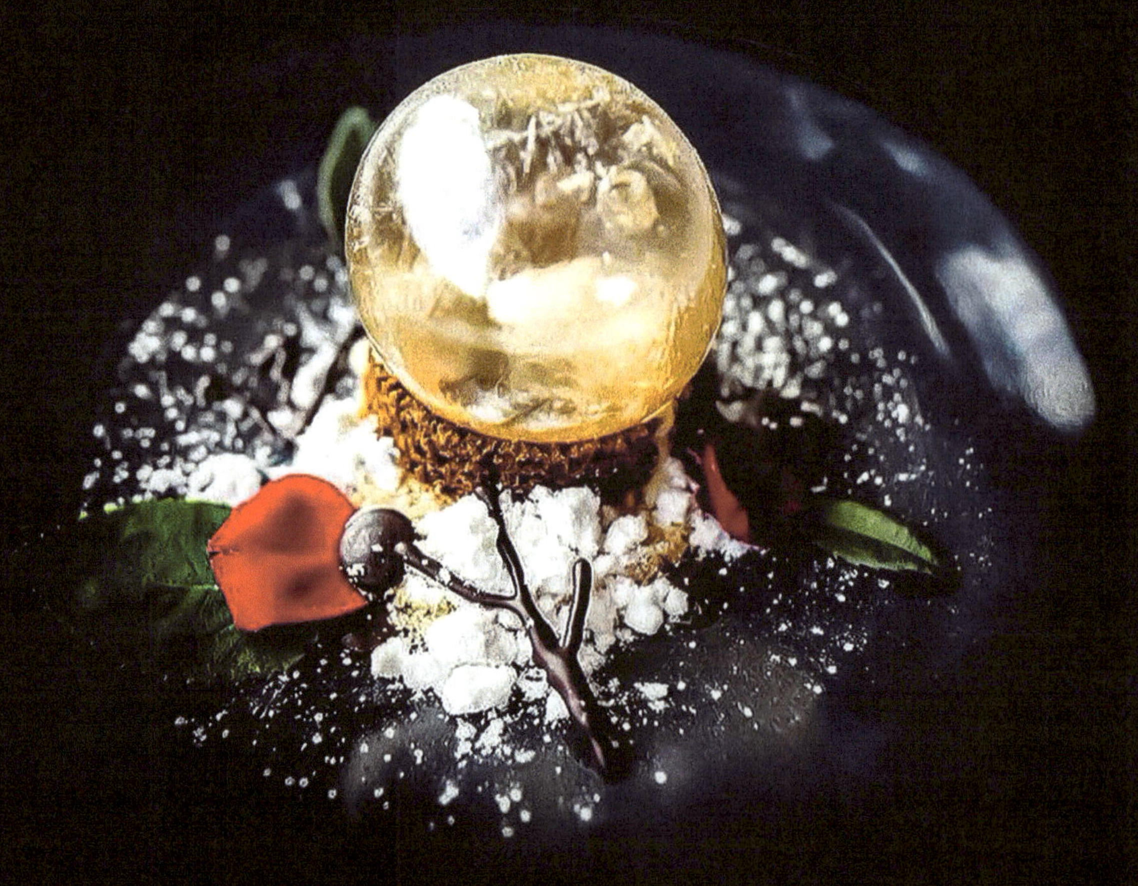

Pain D'espices, Peppermint, Chestnut, Milk Chocolat

'Snow Globe'

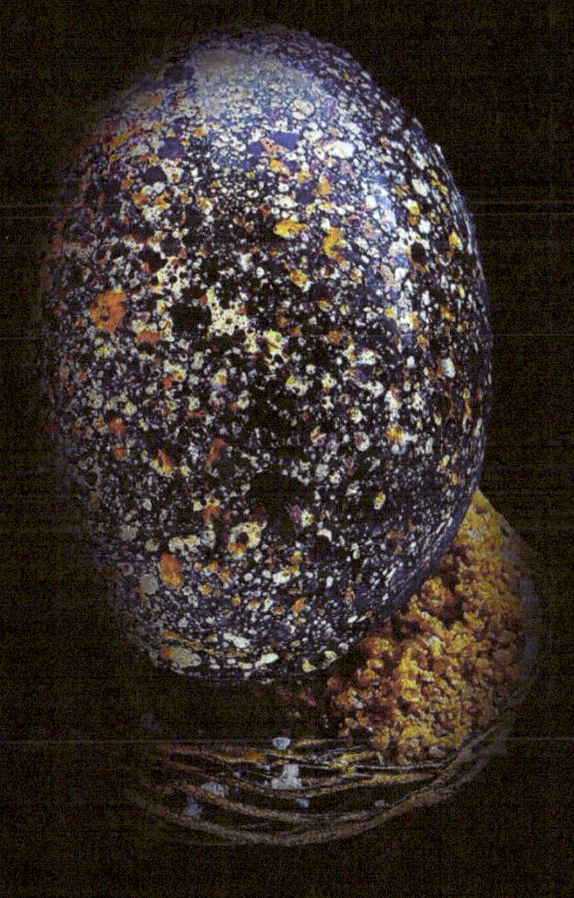

29

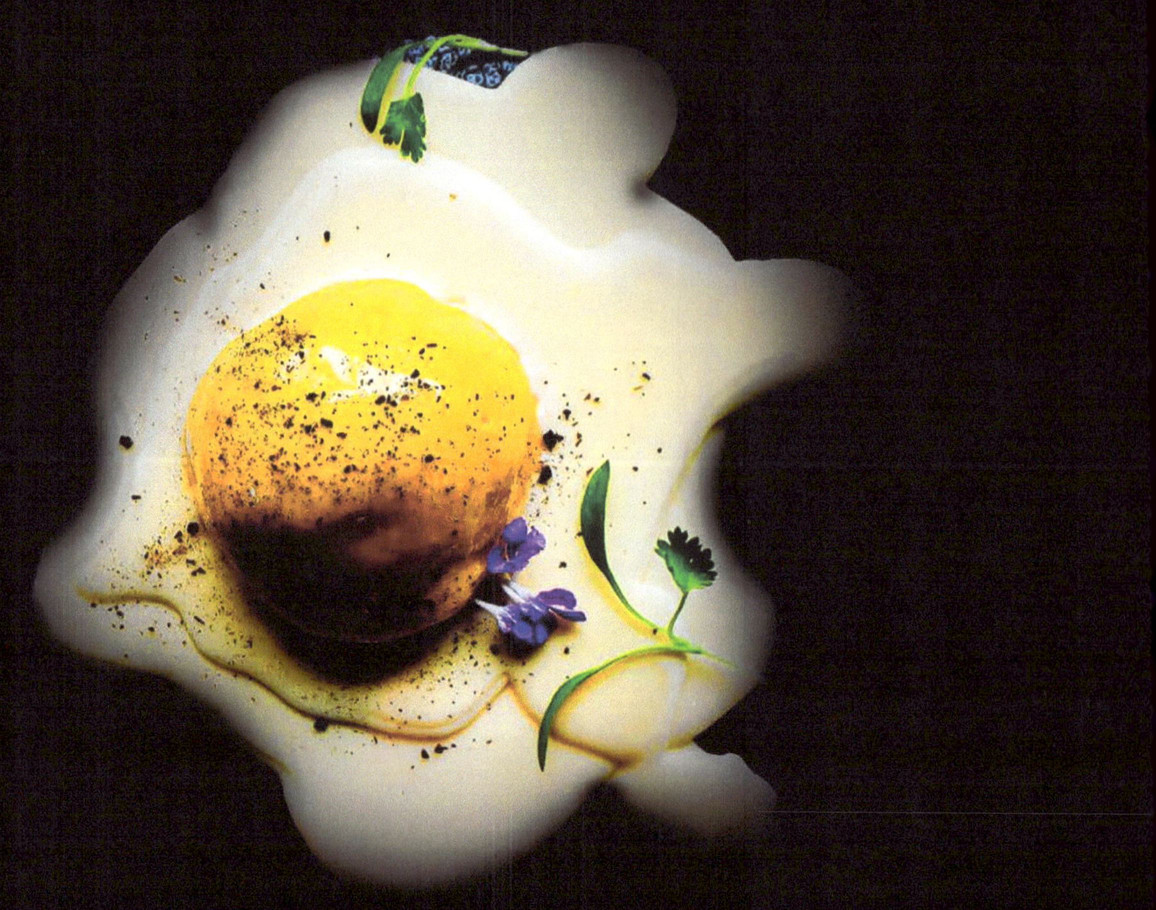

Mango, Black Lime, Coconut, Vanilla

'Egg'

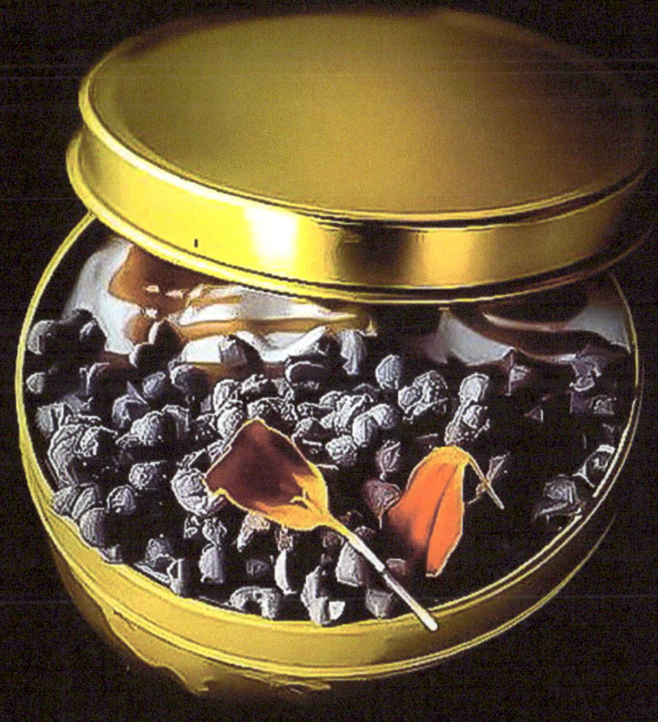

70 Percent Dark Chocolate, Tonka Bean, Vanilla, Espresso

'Affogato Caviar'

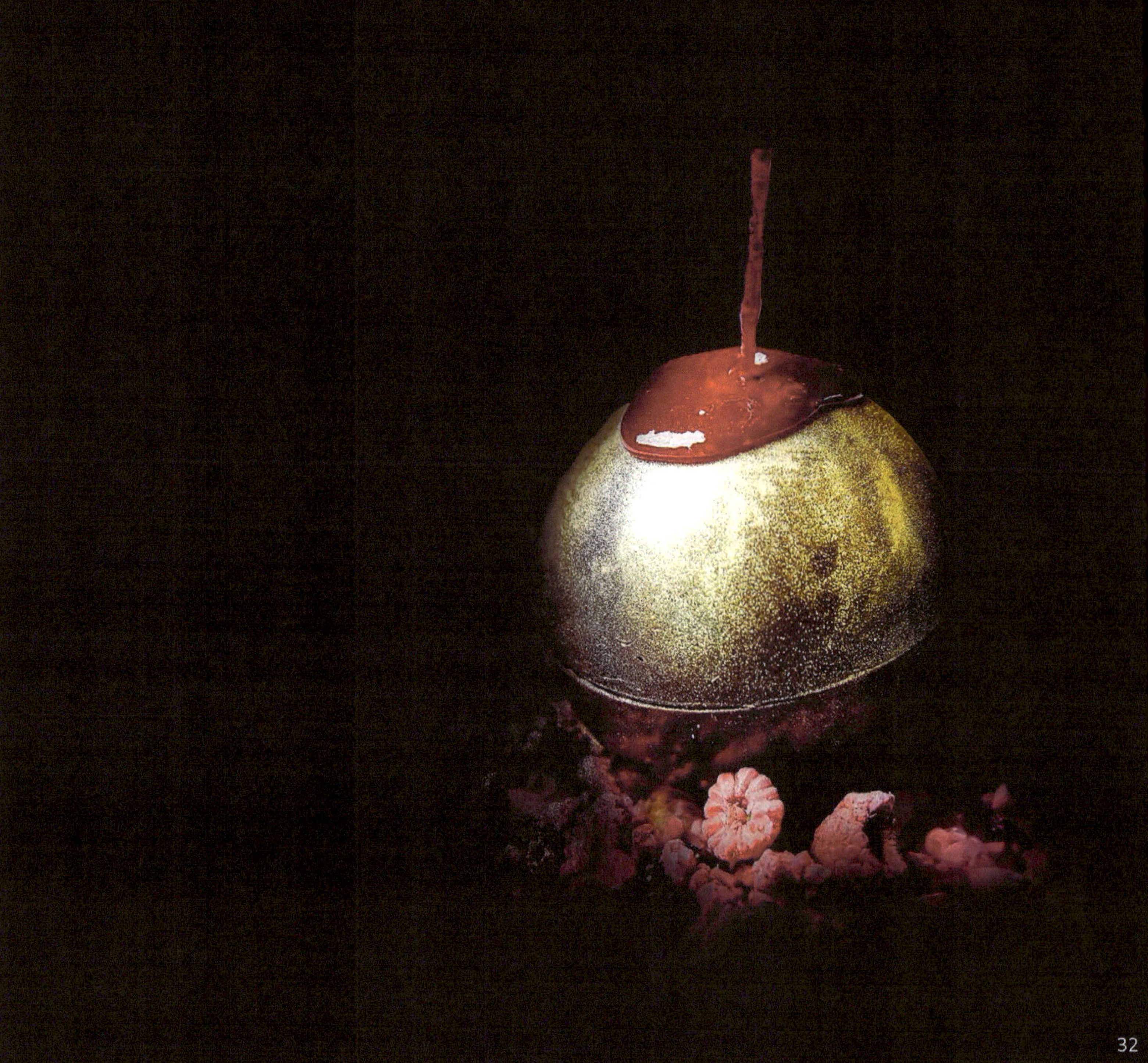

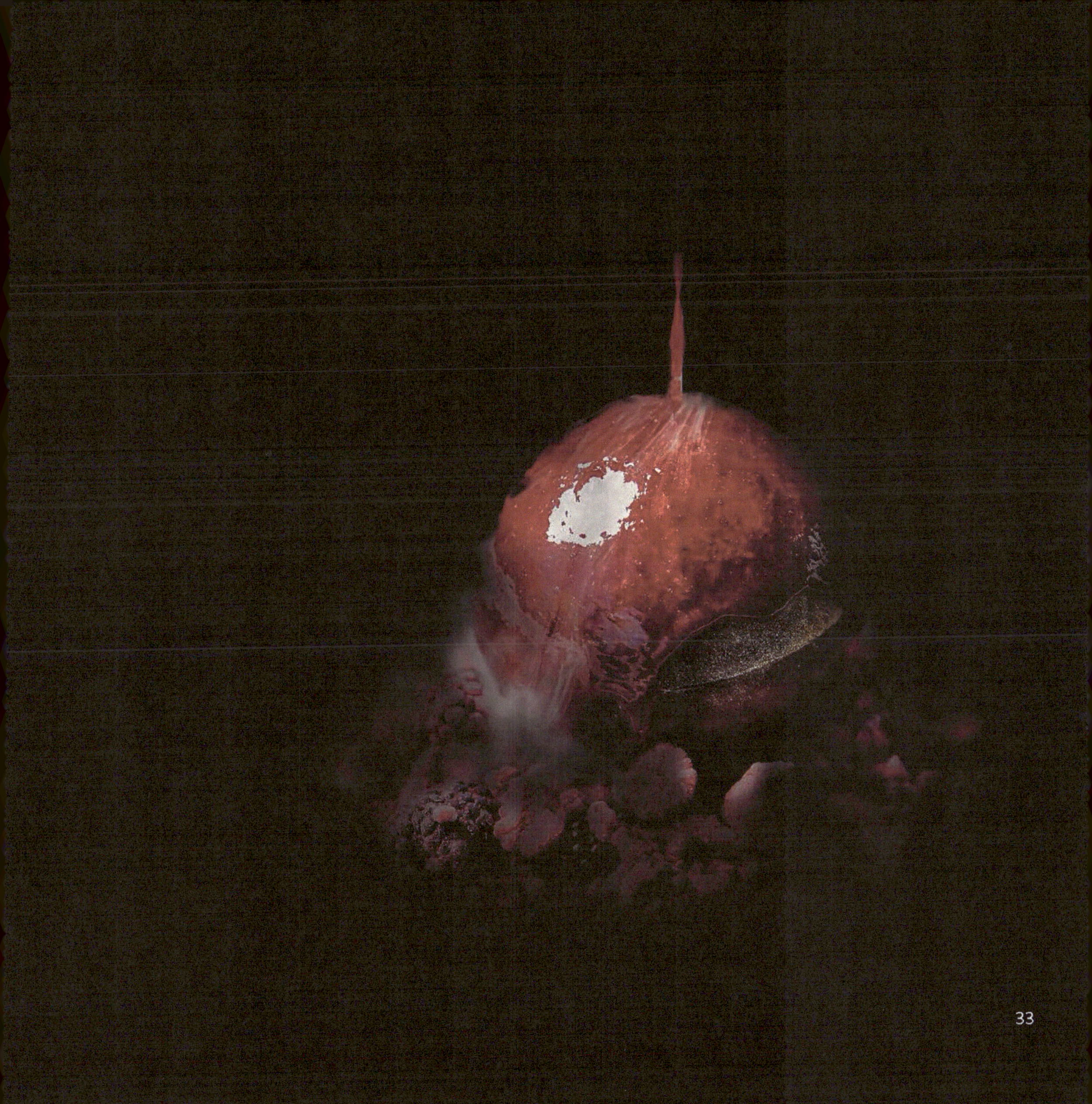

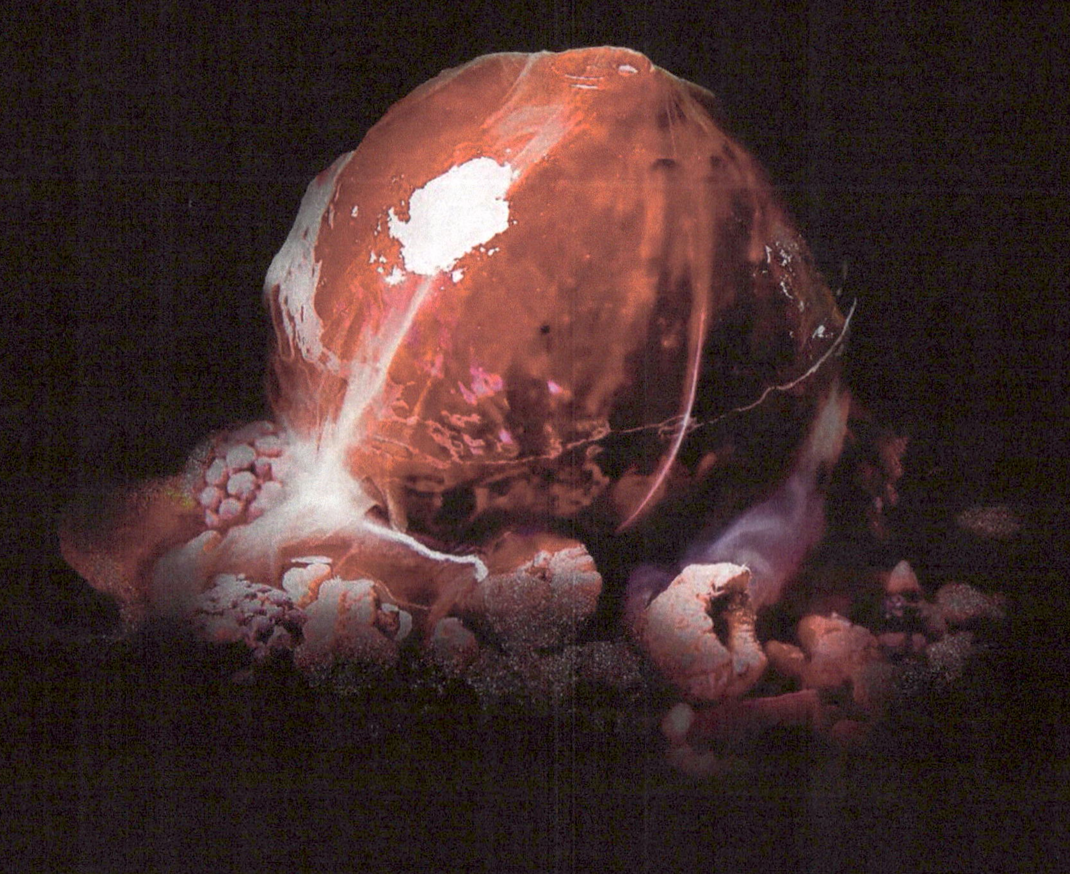

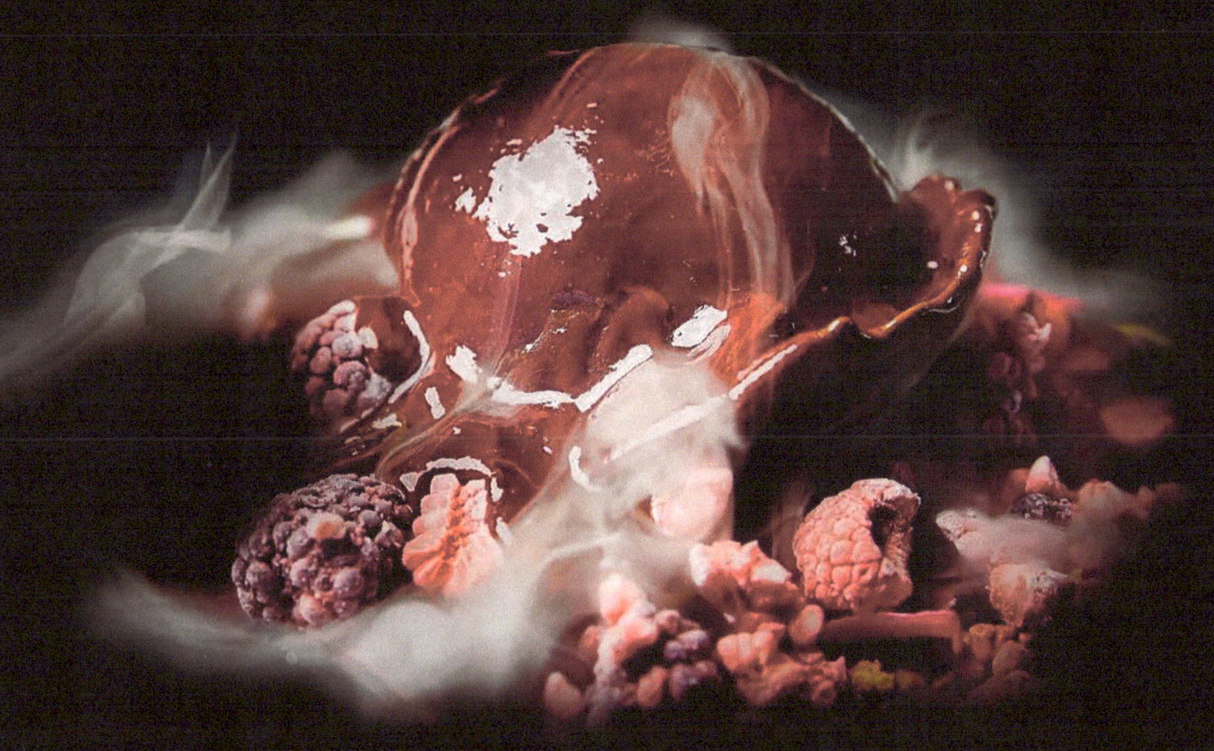

Peanut Butter, Nitro Berries, 38 % Milk Chocolate

'PB Bomb'

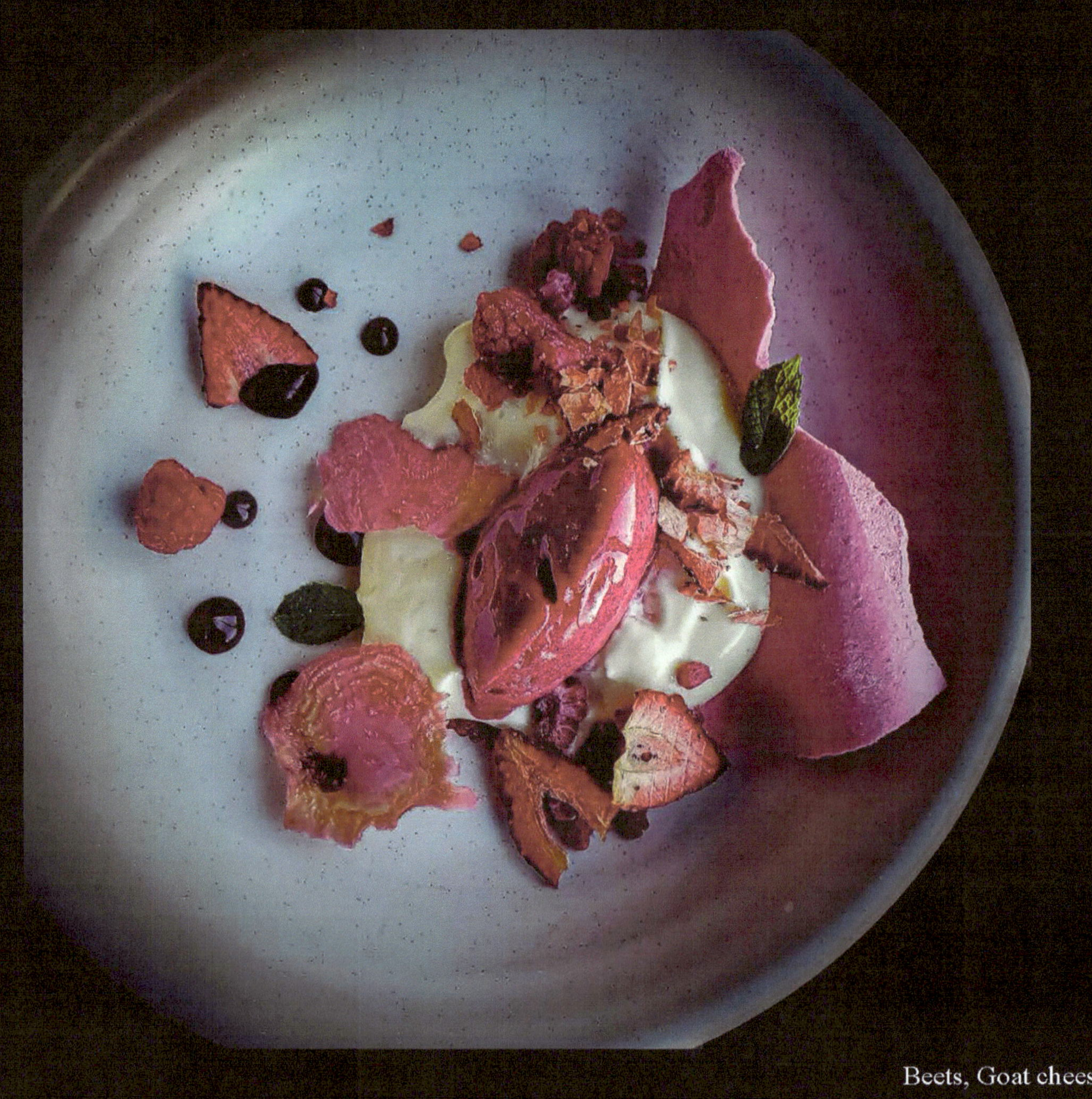

Beets, Goat cheese, Strawberry
"Beets 4 Ways'

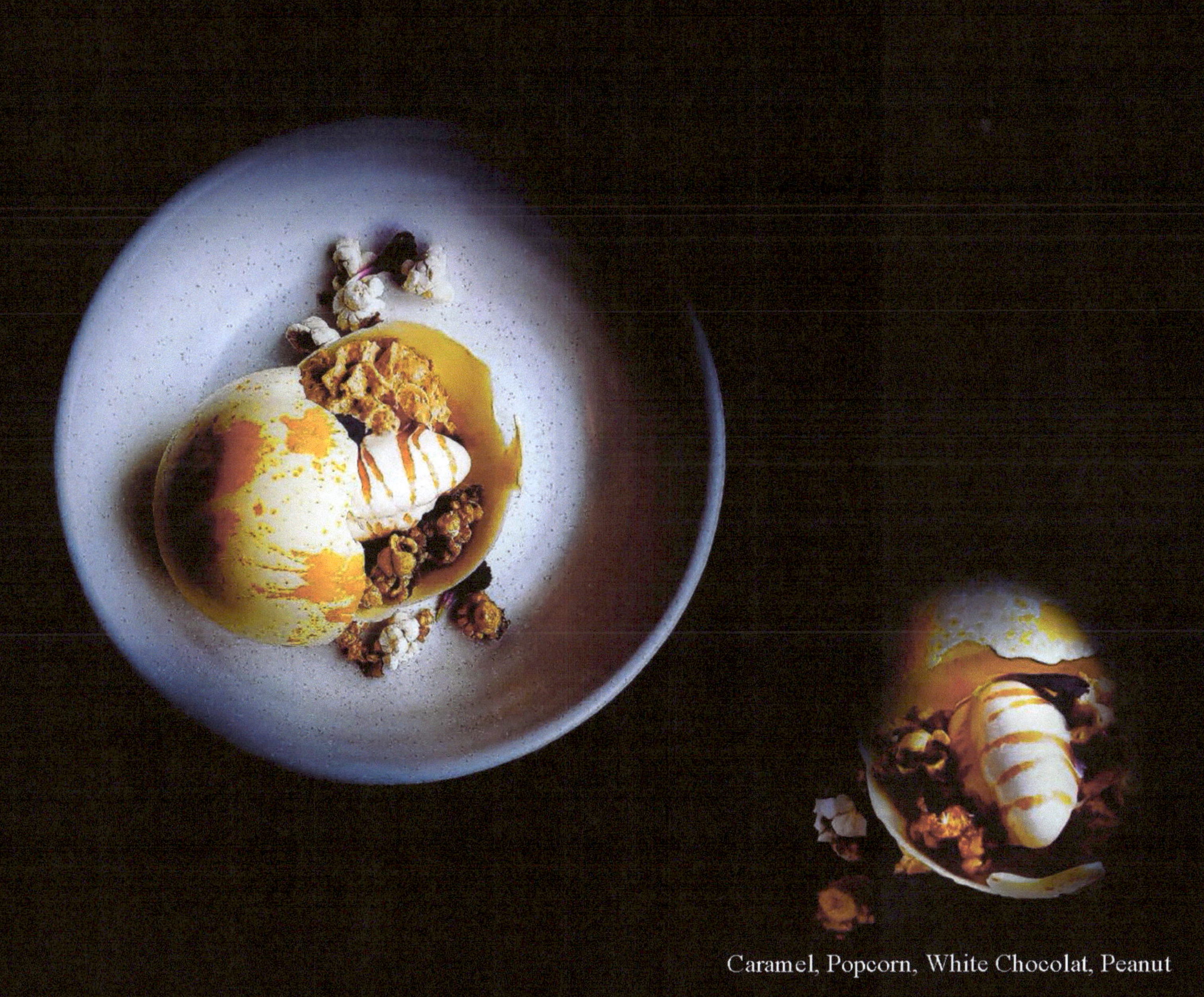

Caramel, Popcorn, White Chocolat, Peanut

'POP'

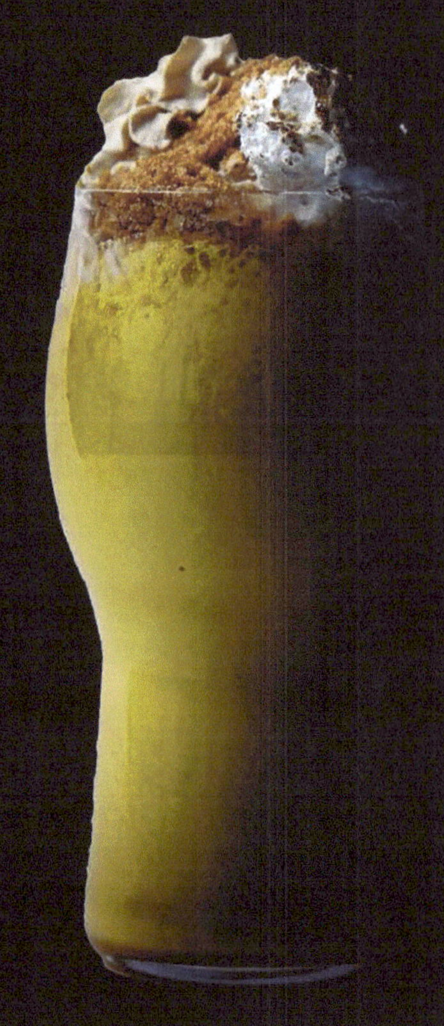

Sweet Potato Pie

Shake   38

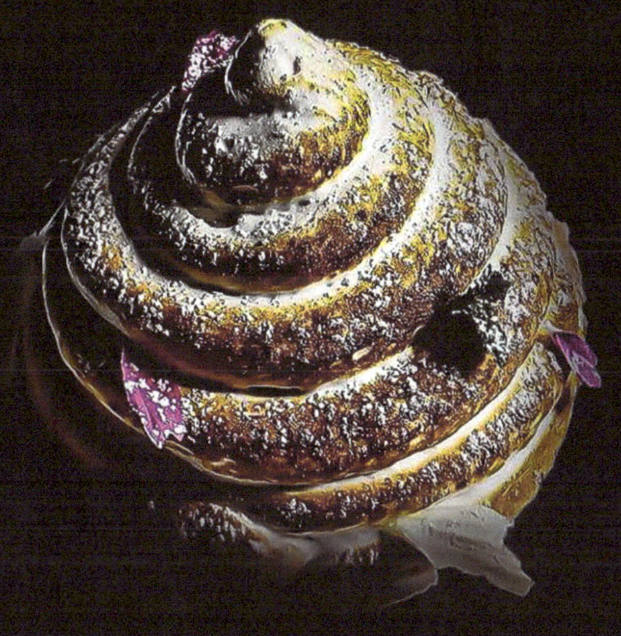

Ube, Blueberry, Black Walnut

'Baked Alaska'

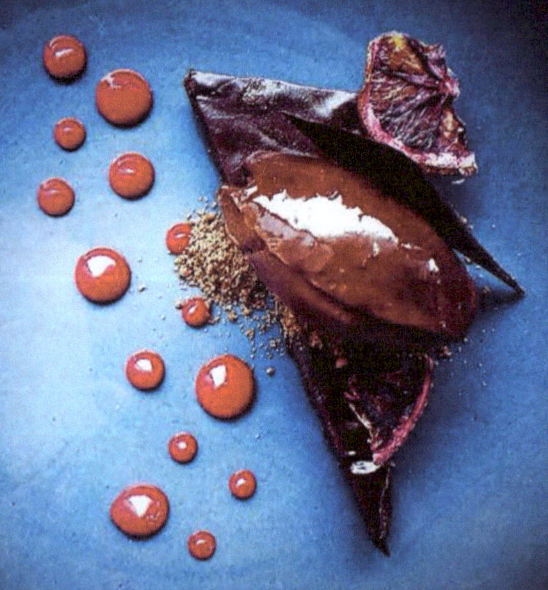

Blood Orange, Dark Chocolate, Sea Salt

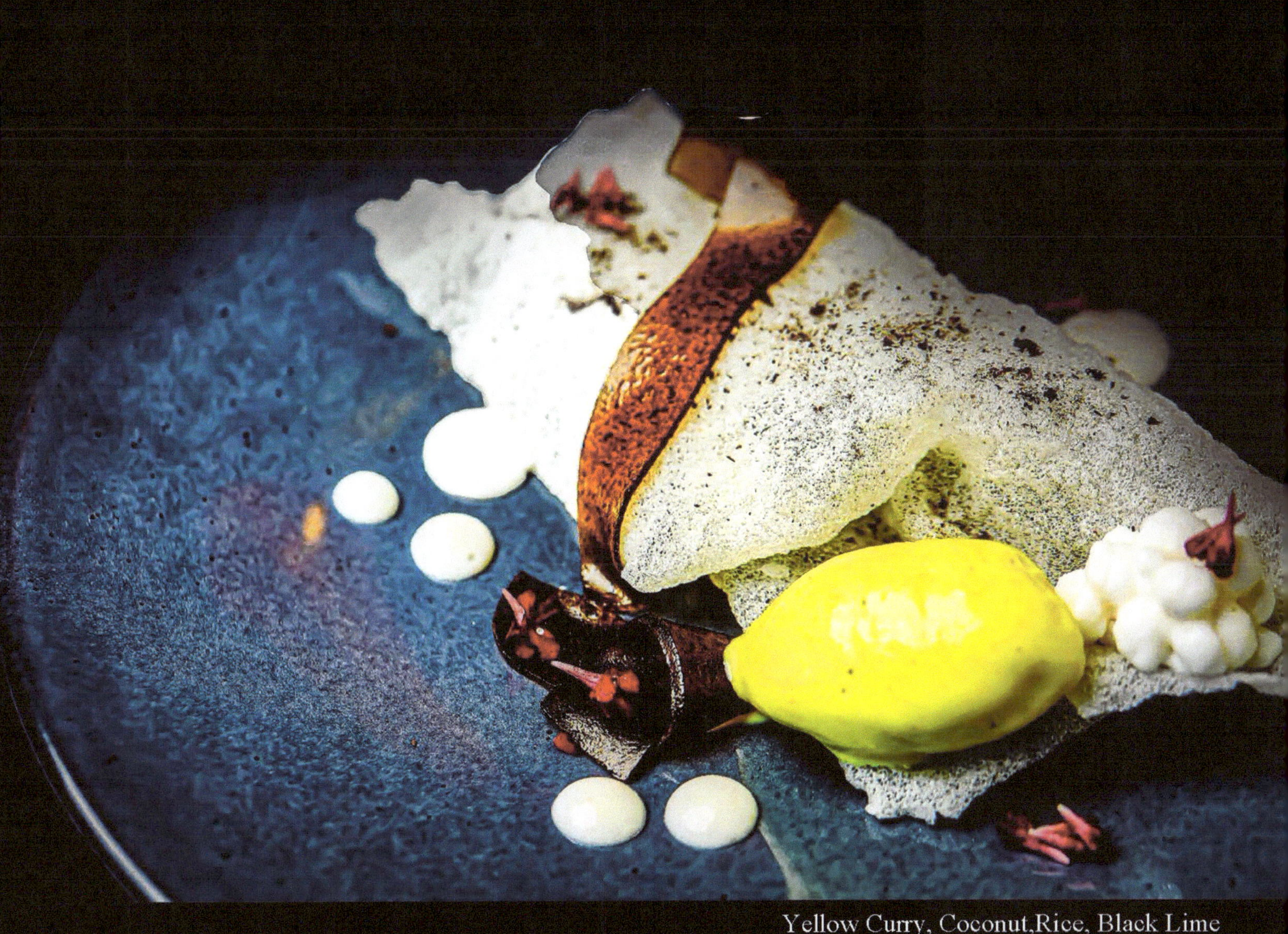

Yellow Curry, Coconut,Rice, Black Lime

Thai Yellow Curry'

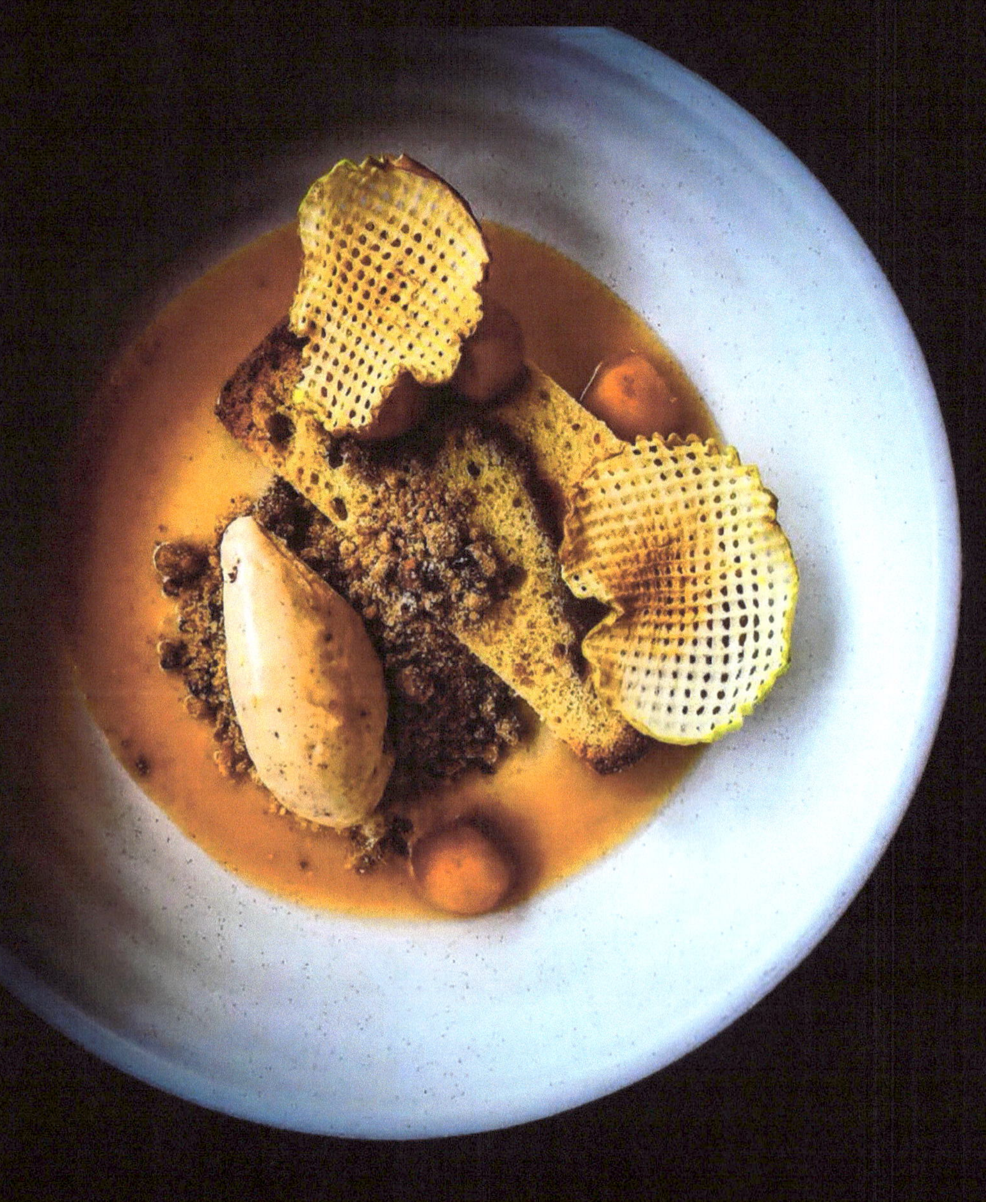

Apple, Whiskey, Spiced Cake, Pecan

'Johnny Apple Seed'

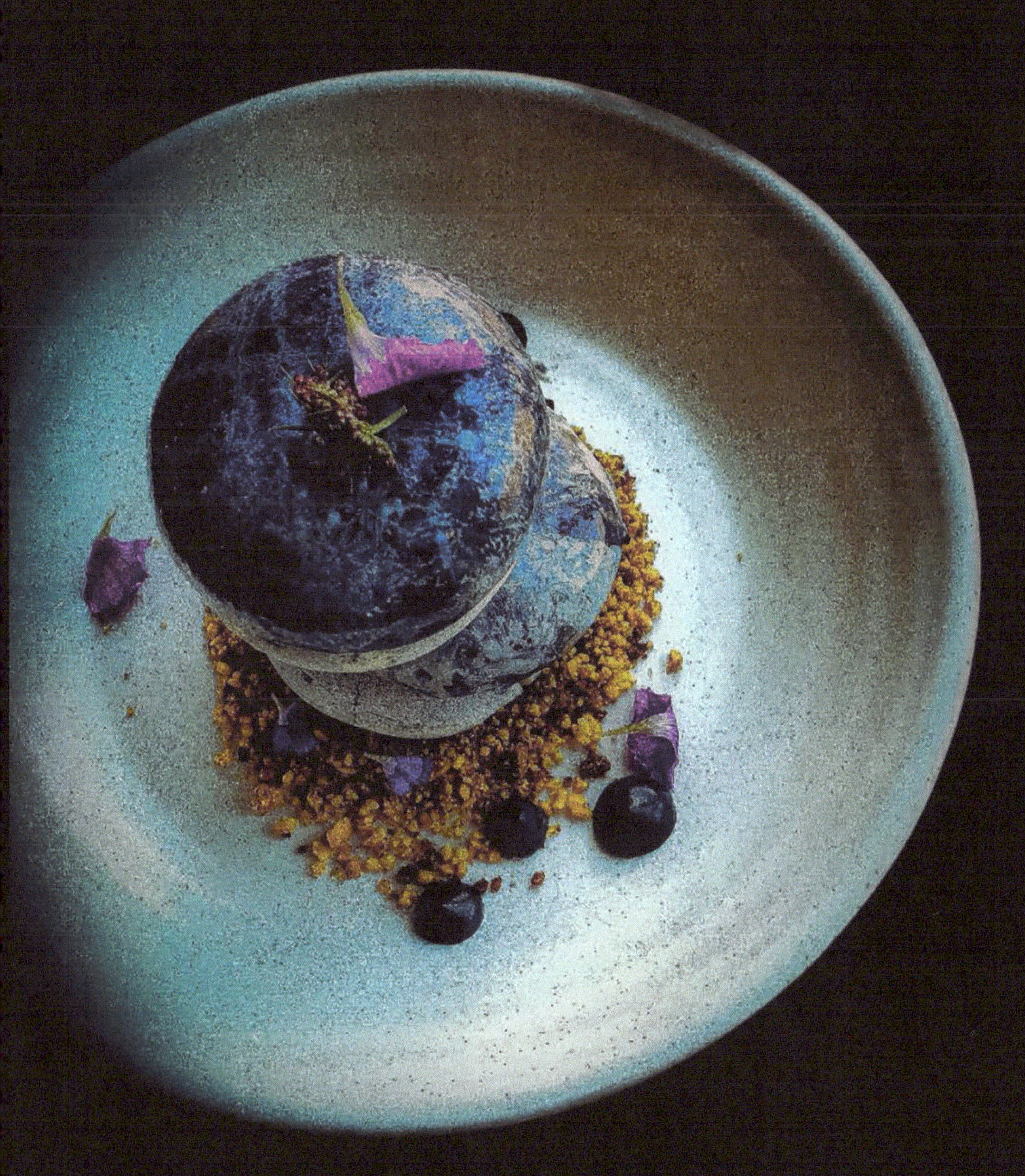

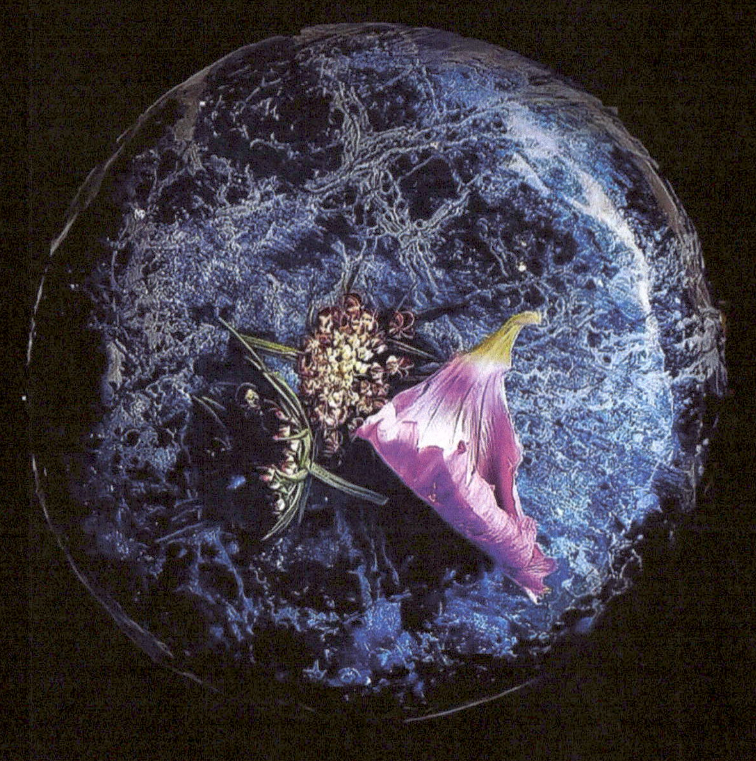

Sesame, White Chocolate, Passion fruit, Miso

'Stones'

'Let the beauty of what you love be what you do.'

[Rumi]

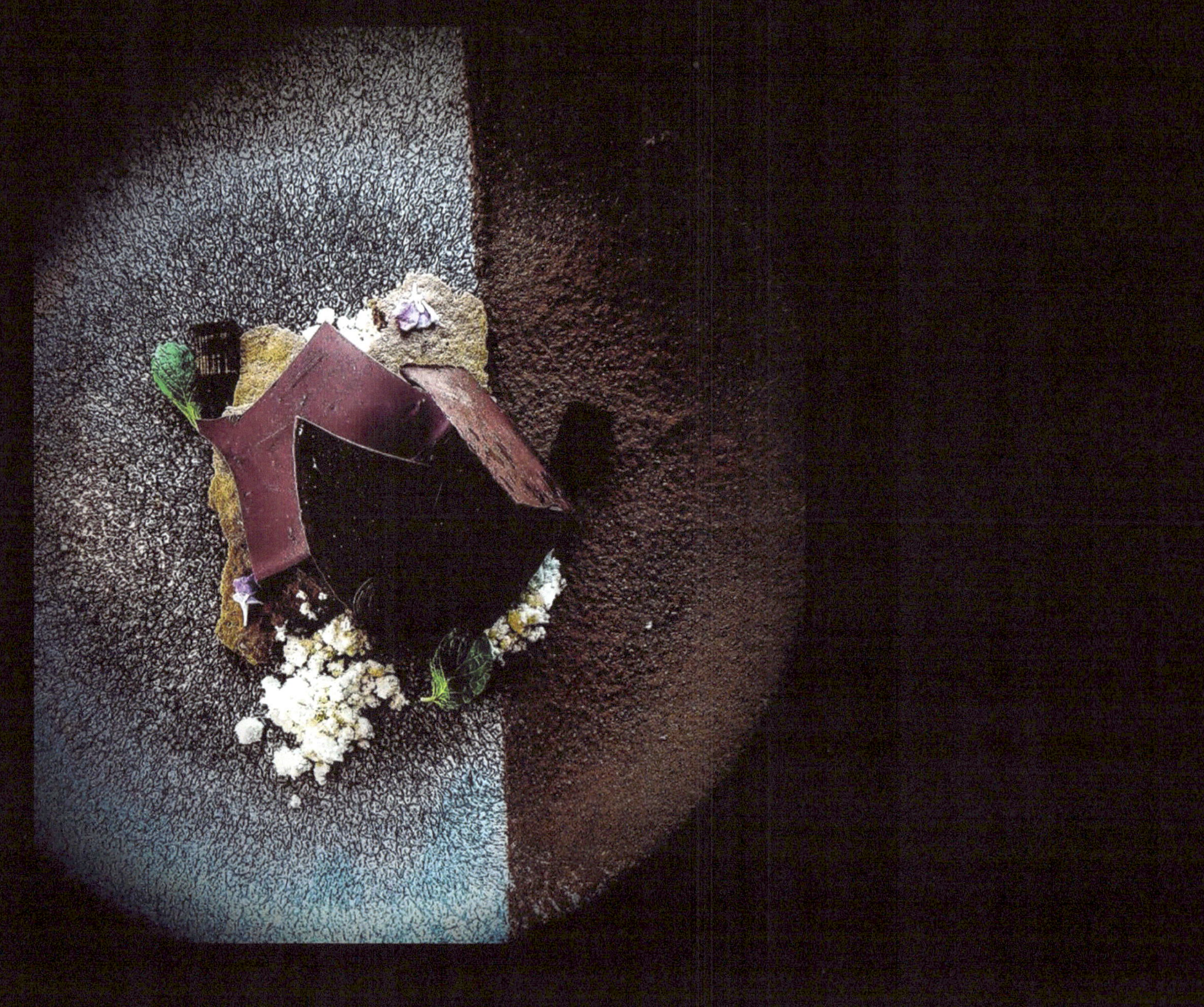

Chocolate-Mint Gelato, Choco-Nib Feuillitine, Nib Gel, Mint Powder, Chocolate Mocha Brownie, Cocoa

'Thin Mint'

Credits

Photography

Tai Davis

pgs. 9, 10,12-14, 18-19, 26, 28-30, 36, 37, 39, 40, 42-44, 46

Judd Demaline

pg. 49

Izaiah Johnson

pgs. 24, 32-35, 38, 41

Wes Law

(Back cover)

Jonathan Pollack 6, 17

Eric Nemens

pgs. 2, 11, 16, 22, 25, 50

Mabel Suen

pg. 31

Food by

Tai Davis

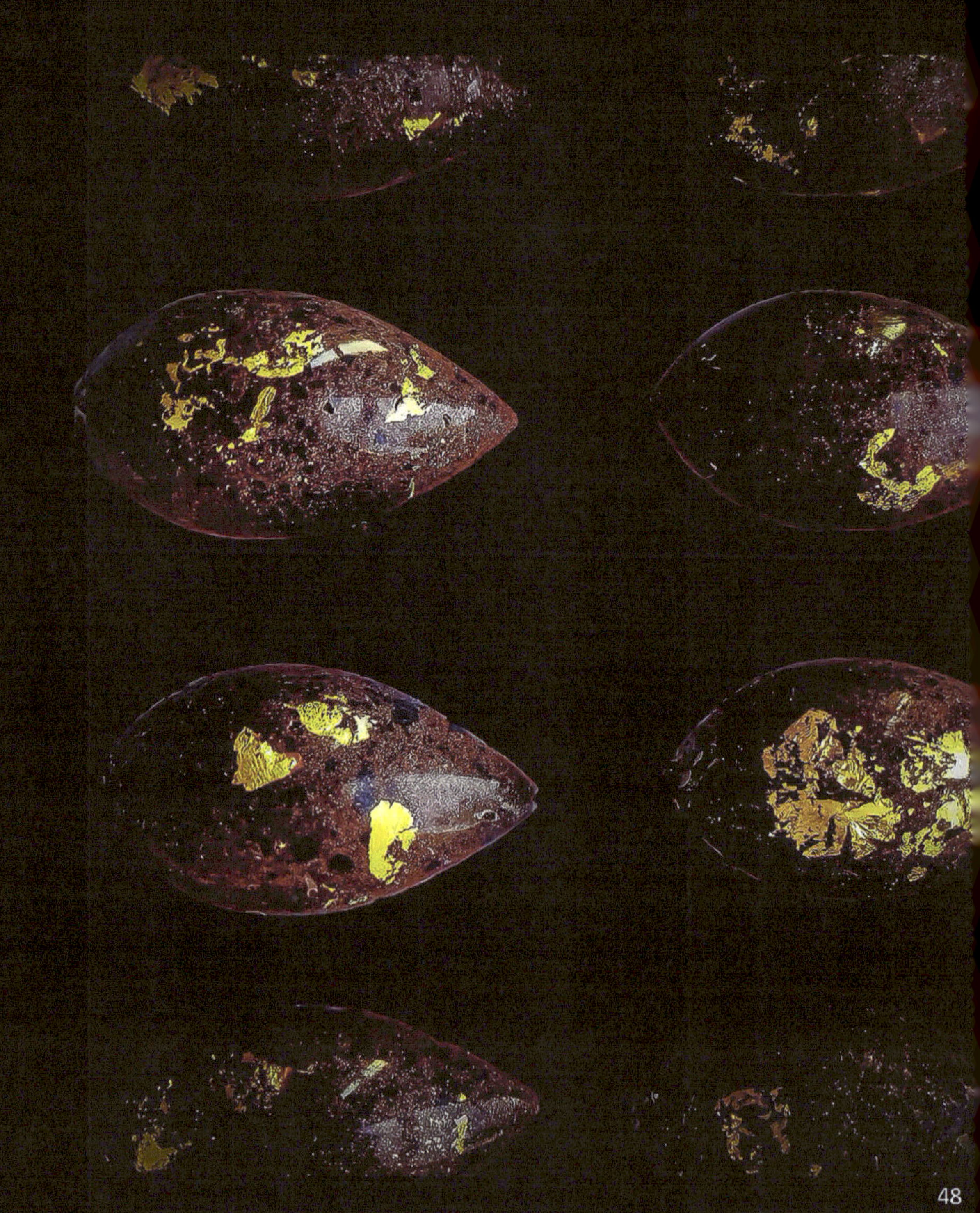

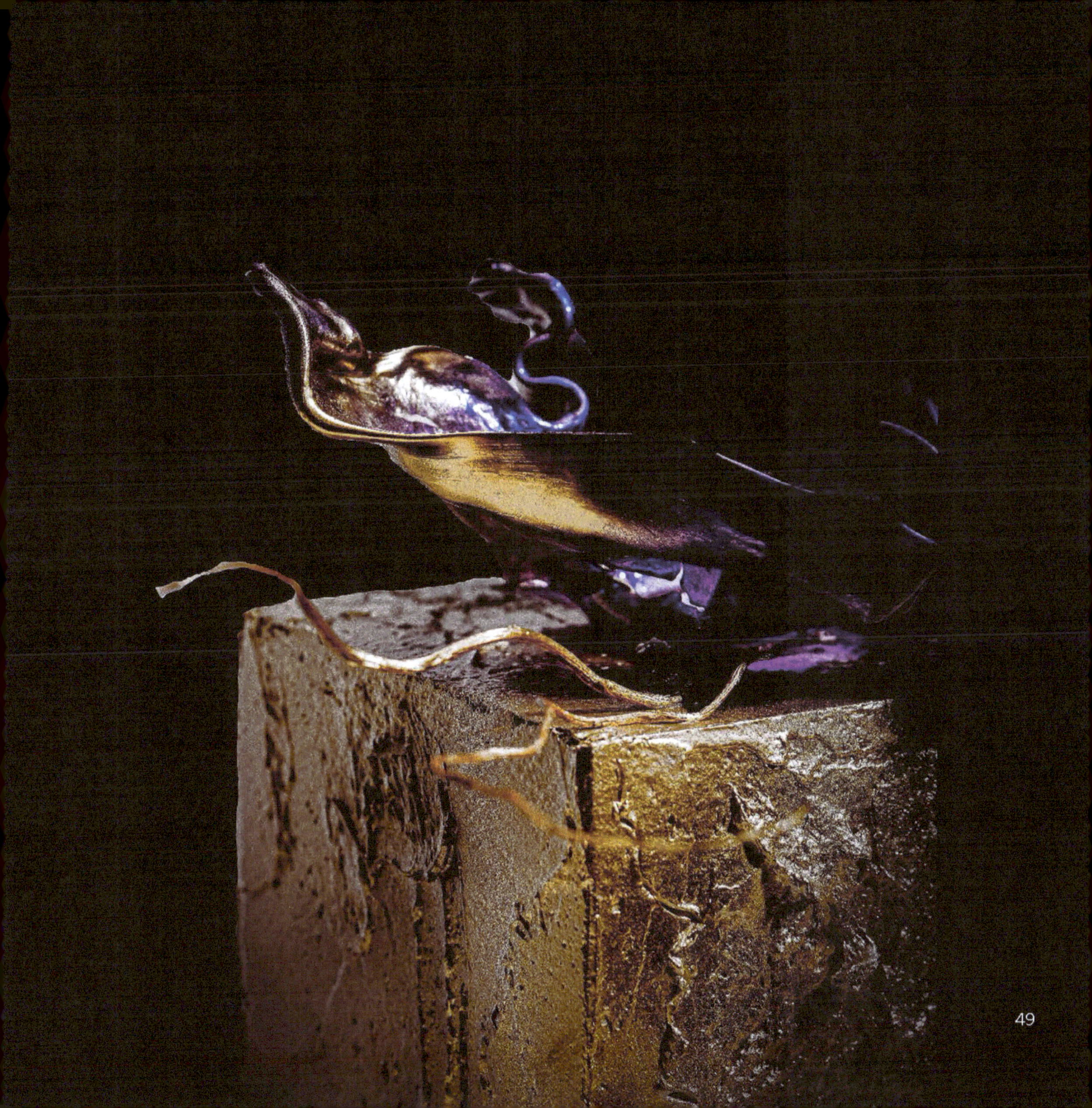

TAI DAVIS [SAVORY]

SUMMER 2020

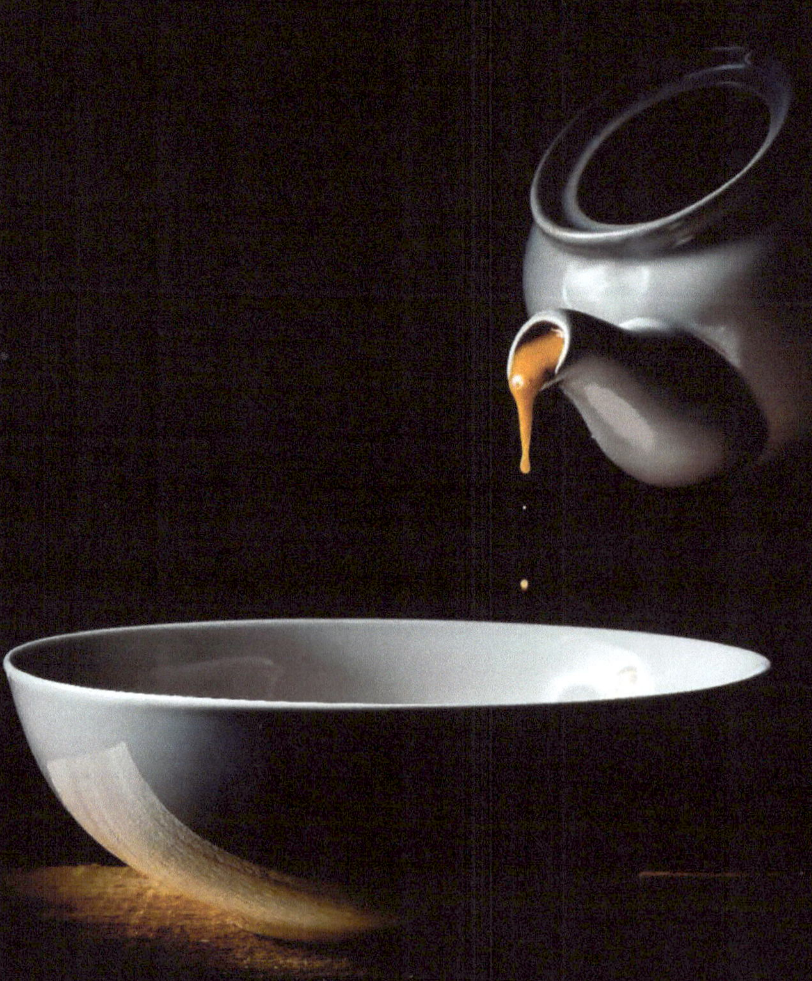

Tyler 'Tai' Davis is one of Saint Louis' brightest rising star chefs. His innovative, and unique aesthetic has earned him accolades from press and public alike.

Tai Davis honed his cooking craft serving as executive chef of The Tavern of Fine Arts in 2017, and as Executive Pastry Chef for The Chocolate Pig Restaurant in 2018. During his tenure at The Chocolate Pig, Chef Tai's culinary prowess has been featured in Sauce, Delta Sky, Feast, E-Squared, Band's Through Town and Saint Louis Magazine. Before his success at The Chocolate Pig, Davis worked and staged in other highly praised kitchens, including Element, The Libertine, Niche, Franco and The Demun Oyster Bar. Most recently, Davis had the opportunity to further showcase his pastry skills on several Food Network competitions.

Currently, Chef Tai has shifted his focus towards consulting, teaching and personal chef services under the moniker Æther. He has also re branded his specialty bakery, Alchemy, and is getting his feet wet in the artistic world as Sacred Geometry by Tai Davis, a concept testing the boundaries between food and art.

Look out for his coffee table book, Tai Davis [Savory], a Visual anthology of recent works, and Solace: Modern Soul Food, coming Summer 2020.